Backpacker's
Pocket Guide

Chris Townsend

 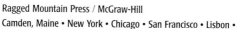 Ragged Mountain Press / McGraw-Hill
Camden, Maine • New York • Chicago • San Francisco • Lisbon •
London • Madrid • Mexico City • Milan • New Delhi • San Juan •
Seoul• Singapore • Sydney • Toronto

W9-DAF-459

Look for these other Ragged Mountain Press Pocket Guides:

Edible Wild Plants and Herbs, Alan M. Cvancara
Sea Kayaker's Pocket Guide, Shelley Johnson
Wilderness First Aid, Paul G. Gill Jr., M.D.

Ragged Mountain Press
A Division of The McGraw-Hill Companies

10 9 8 7 6 5 4 3 2 1

Questions regarding the content of this book should be addressed to
Ragged Mountain Press
P.O. Box 220
Camden, ME 04843
www.raggedmountainpress.com

Questions regarding the ordering of this book should be addressed to
The McGraw-Hill Companies
Customer Service Department
P.O. Box 547
Blacklick, OH 43004
Retail customers: 1-800-262-4729
Bookstores: 1-800-722-4726

This book is printed on 60# Citation by R. R. Donnelley

Photographs by the author except for the following: page 96 Cliff Leight; pages 12, 22, 60–61, 106, 118, 122 Corbis Images; pages 6–7, 109, 119 Digital Stock; page 86 John Laptad/The Coleman Company.

Illustrations by Chris Hoyt; running foot illustration by Matt Watier; Design by Geri Davis, Davis Associates, and Anton Marc; Page layout by Janet Robbins; Edited by Tom McCarthy, Jonathan Eaton, and Kathryn Thompson.

Contents

Campcraft

First Aid

Introduction

Practicalities are the bedrock of backpacking. Get them right, and you can enjoy the wilderness in all its glory. Many books give advice on various aspects of backpacking, from choosing a tent to deciding which trail to hike. I've written a couple myself. But you wouldn't want to carry these books in your pack, since much of the information isn't stuff you need when you're actually out in the wilds. That's where this book comes in. It's light enough to carry and contains just the practical information you need on the trail and in camp. If you want information on choosing gear or planning a hike, this isn't the book for you (for that material, have a look at my *Backpacker's Handbook* and *The Advanced Backpacker*). But if you want to know what to do when your stove jams or how to keep warm in camp or dry on the trail, this book will tell you.

Backpacking isn't about stove maintenance and keeping warm, though—it's about reveling in striding over a mountain pass and wandering along a forest trail, about watching the sun rise over distant mountains or a rainbow appear as a storm fades away. The advice in this book is designed to let you do just that by helping you sort out the functional stuff as quickly and efficiently as possible.

San Gabriel Mountains, California

Acknowledgments

I have to admit that the idea for this book wasn't mine. Two people came up with it separately. First was my partner, Denise Thorn, who said she'd like a portable book containing just the practical, on-trail advice from my other books on backpacking. Then Tom McCarthy of Ragged Mountain Press approached me and suggested a guidebook for "quick, on-trail access." My thanks to both of them. Denise also checked the text and assured me that this was the information she was seeking. I am of course responsible for the contents and any errors.

All the people thanked in my other backpacking books deserve credit here as this material is contained in those books in much more detail and with much else besides. I won't list them again here. This is meant to be a lightweight book!

I would, though, like to thank the people at Ragged Mountain Press who have worked hard to make this book what it is.

Backpacking Basics

BEFORE YOU GO

WHAT TO TAKE

On any trip you need shelter, suitable clothing, sustenance, and a pack to carry these things.

To ensure that you don't forget anything, it's best to work from a checklist. Here is a basic one covering all the items you might want on a trip. Of course, weather and trip duration will affect which items you ultimately decide to carry. On most trips you'll bring only a selection of this gear. A pared down checklist for a short hike (one to two days) in a temperate climate is included to show what a minimal list might look like. During and after a hike it's worth making notes on what gear you needed, what you didn't use, and what you could have done without. The lighter your load, the more enjoyable the hike.

CHECKLIST

Carriage and Storage

Pack with cover
Fanny pack
Stuff sacks

Shelter and Sleeping

Tent with fly sheet, poles, and
    stakes
Tarp
Bivouac bag
Ground cloth
Sleeping bag
Sleeping bag liner
Insulating mat (sleeping pad
    or mattress)

Kitchen Gear

Stove
Windscreen
Fuel
Pouring spout or eyedropper
    for fuel
Pan(s) with lid(s)
Mug
Plate or bowl

Spoons
Pot holder
Dishcloth or sponge
Water containers
Water purification tablets or
    drops
Water filter
Spare water filter cartridge
Matches or lighter
Plastic bags, various sizes
Bear bag (stuff sack) and hang-
    ing rope
Bear-resistant container
Food (see pages 90, 96–97)

Clothing

Inner layer
Synthetic T-shirt
Synthetic wicking shirt
Long underwear
Long-sleeved trail shirt
Underpants
Sports bra

Upper-body insulating layer
Thick shirt
Pile/fleece/wool vest, sweater,
    or jacket
Insulated vest, sweater, or
    jacket

Outer layer
Windproof shirt or jacket
Rain jacket
Rain pants

Legwear
Shorts
Trail pants
Fleece/pile pants

Footwear
Boots or trail shoes
Camp shoes or sandals
Socks (not cotton)
Liner socks

Headwear
Sun hat
Waterproof hat
Knit hat
Neck gaiter
Balaclava
Pile-lined cap

Mitts and gloves
Liner gloves
Wool/pile mittens or gloves
Overmitts or gloves

Lighting
Flashlight or headlamp
Spare flashlight bulb and
    batteries
Candles
Candle lantern
Oil lantern
Pressure lantern

Navigation Aids
Compass
Map
Map case or resealable bag
Trail guide
Barometer (altimeter)
GPS receiver

Repair Kit
Ripstop nylon patches
Duct tape
Needles and thread
Awl
Urethane adhesive
Stove maintenance kit or jet
    pricker
Rubber bands
Length of adhesive-backed
    Velcro
Self-inflating mattress repair kit
Spare pack buckles
Spare clevis pins for pack
Wire or paper clips

First-Aid Kit
First-aid booklet
2nd Skin/Compeed
Elastic/crepe bandage
1-inch adhesive tape
Nonabsorbent bandages for
    burns
Antiseptic wipes
Assorted Band-Aids
Steri-Strips
Safety pins
Rubbing alcohol wipes
Foil-wrapped painkillers
Antihistamine
Scissors (may be on knife)
Tweezers (may be on knife)
Sawyer Extractor snakebite kit
Tick removal kit
Latex gloves
Personal medication as needed
Antihistamine or other allergy
    medication as needed

Card for notes in case of an accident or illness and pencil

Miscellaneous Tools and Gear

Umbrella
Staff or hiking poles
Spare tips for hiking poles
Safety whistle
Signal mirror
Waterproof/windproof matches
Washkit (toothbrush, toothpaste, biodegradable soap, tampons, etc.)
Towel
Sunglasses
Spare eyeglasses or contacts
Sunscreen
Lip balm-sunscreen
Insect repellent
Mosquito coils
Head net
Bear-repellent spray
Flares
Cell phone
Rope
Parachute cord
Pocket knife
Notebook, pen, and documents (trail permit, identification, travel tickets) in waterproof nylon pouch or plastic bag
Watch
Toilet trowel
Toilet paper
Bandanna

Miscellaneous Extras

Binoculars
Photography Equipment
  cameras
  lenses
  flash
  spare batteries
  tripod
  mini-tripod/clamp
  filters
  cable release
  lens tissue
  film
  padded camera cases
Paperback book(s)
Playing cards
Games
Radio
Personal stereo
Thermometer

Snow and Winter Extras

Ice ax
Crampons
Snowshoes
Skis
Ski poles
Ski boots
Climbing skins
Ski wax
Insulated booties
Gaiters
Insulated gloves
Snow goggles

Lake McDonald, Glacier National Park, Montana

CHECKLIST FOR A SHORT TRIP IN MODERATE WEATHER

- ❑ Pack with cover
- ❑ Stuff sacks
- ❑ Tent with fly sheet, poles, and stakes, or tarp
- ❑ Sleeping bag
- ❑ Insulating mat (sleeping pad)
- ❑ Stove
- ❑ Fuel
- ❑ Pan(s) with lid(s)
- ❑ Mug
- ❑ Plate or bowl unless solo
- ❑ Spoon(s)
- ❑ Dishcloth or sponge
- ❑ Water containers
- ❑ Water purification tablets/ drops or water filter
- ❑ Spare water filter cartridge
- ❑ Matches or lighter
- ❑ Plastic bags, various sizes
- ❑ Bear bag (stuff sack) and hanging rope (only if going into bear country)
- ❑ Food (see pages 90, 96–97)
- ❑ Synthetic T-shirt
- ❑ Long-sleeved trail shirt
- ❑ Underpants
- ❑ Sports bra
- ❑ Pile/fleece/wool vest, sweater, or jacket
- ❑ Windproof shirt or jacket
- ❑ Rain jacket
- ❑ Rain pants
- ❑ Shorts
- ❑ Fleece/pile pants
- ❑ Boots or trail shoes
- ❑ Camp shoes or sandals
- ❑ Socks (not cotton)
- ❑ Sun hat
- ❑ Warm hat
- ❑ Flashlight or headlamp
- ❑ Spare flashlight bulb and batteries
- ❑ Compass
- ❑ Map
- ❑ Map case or resealable bag
- ❑ Trail guide
- ❑ Duct tape
- ❑ Needles and thread
- ❑ Length of adhesive-backed Velcro
- ❑ Elastic/crepe bandage
- ❑ 1-inch adhesive tape
- ❑ Antiseptic wipes
- ❑ Assorted Band-Aids
- ❑ Foil-wrapped painkillers
- ❑ Personal medication as needed
- ❑ Antihistamine or other allergy medication as needed
- ❑ Hiking pole(s)
- ❑ Safety whistle
- ❑ Signal mirror (opt.)
- ❑ Waterproof/windproof matches
- ❑ Washkit (toothbrush, toothpaste, biodegradable soap, tampons, etc.)
- ❑ Towel (opt.)
- ❑ Sunglasses
- ❑ Sunscreen
- ❑ Insect repellent
- ❑ Rope or parachute cord (opt.)
- ❑ Pocket knife
- ❑ Notebook, pen, and documents (trail permit, identification, travel tickets) in waterproof nylon pouch or plastic bag
- ❑ Watch
- ❑ Toilet trowel
- ❑ Bandanna
- ❑ Binoculars (opt.)
- ❑ Camera

LEAVE A PLAN BEHIND

Leave your itinerary with someone reliable—friend, family member, land management official—so if you fail to return by a certain time a search can be organized. Include as much information as possible, including alternative bad-weather routes or plans. Make sure you agree on the exact time the authorities should be notified if you haven't been in touch. For long trips include details of supply points and approximate dates you'll make contact by phone.

Once your trip is over, always make contact as soon as possible. Too many searches have been carried out for people who were sitting in a café or on a beach somewhere and hadn't bothered to let their contact person know they were safe.

Itinerary

Members of party: Chris, Dan, Molly, Jon, Denise . . . .

Day, time, and location of departure: Monday, July 23, 7:00 am . . . . .

Car(s), license plate number, location, and description: blue Subaru station wagon, Maine PACK-IT plate @ Baxter State Park, Roaring Brook campground . . . .

Day, time, and location of return: Wednesday, July 27, 3 pm, Roaring Brook Ranger's Station . . . .

Cell phone number. . . . .

Day: July 23 . . . . . Planned route: Abol Trail to Baxter Peak to Chimney Pond. . . . .

Day: July 24 . . . . . Planned route: Chimney Pond to Roaring Brook. .

Day: July 25 . . . . . Planned route: Roaring Brook to Russell Pond. . .

Day: July 26 . . . . . Planned route: Russell Pond to North Brother Gap

Day: July 27 . . . . . Planned route: North Brother Gap to Nesowadnehunk Stream Campground . . . .

Will call to check in: 6 pm. . . . .

If not back by 8 pm . . . . notify Nesowadnehunk Ranger's Station

---

TRAILHEAD CAR SAFETY

Leaving a vehicle at a trailhead for days at a time may be risky. If you have to do so, find out in advance from the local police, rangers, or hiking club whether any of the possible trailheads are known for break-ins, damage, or vehicle theft. Ask a local business, such as a motel, gas station, or restaurant, if you may leave your car in their parking lot. Ask the local outfitter or hiking club about getting to the trailhead—some popular trailheads have shuttles. You could also take a taxi to the trailhead or pay someone local to drive you there.

If you must leave a car at the trailhead, park in an open area with the trunk facing into the parking lot. The more visible your vehicle, the less attractive it is to thieves. And the more expensive your vehicle, the more likely it is to attract attention. Don't leave valuables in the car. Take money and car keys with you—thieves know all the possible hiding places. Store anything else of value out of sight—this makes it less *likely* to be stolen, but that's all. Don't leave anything in a vehicle you're not prepared to lose. Thieves may watch parking lots to see who puts items worth stealing into the trunk or under seats.

Sign in at trailhead registers, but don't leave a note on your dashboard or in the window of your vehicle saying where you've gone and when you'll be back. It simply tells thieves how long they've got.

HEADING OUT

PACKING

Your pack must be properly packed in order for you to carry it comfortably. If at any point during a hike your pack feels uncomfortable or lopsided, stop and repack it.

For trail hiking, carrying the weight up high lets you walk upright. Light bulky items such as sleeping bags and clothing go low in the pack; heavy, relatively low-bulk items such as food go near the top. Keep heavy items close to your back to prevent the pack from pulling backward, forcing you to lean forward.

For off-trail hiking on rough ground, where balance is especially important, place heavier items in the middle rather than

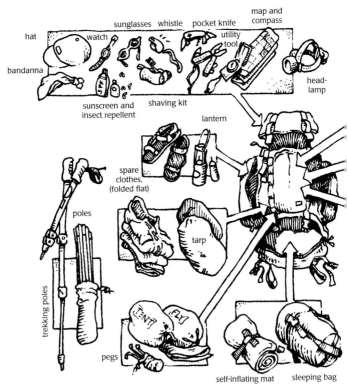

This shows all the things you might carry, but you'll never need all of it on one trip.

at the top, still as close to the back as possible, as this makes for a more stable pack. (Women may prefer packs loaded like this even on trails, due to their lower center of gravity.)

Keeping items in stuff sacks helps keep your pack organized and makes things easier to find. Items that may be needed during the day can go in external pockets or at the top of the main compartment for quick accessibility without having to unpack other gear.

If rain is at all likely, line your pack with a garbage bag or else use a pack cover: few packs are fully waterproof.

The illustration (left) shows a good way to load a pack with two compartments, a lid pocket, and two side or rear pockets.

If it's wet the shelter goes in last, inside a waterproof bag so it won't soak the other contents.

All these items can be moved around depending on the layout of the pack. Heavy items like full water or fuel bottles or bags of food are best not carried in rear pockets, however.

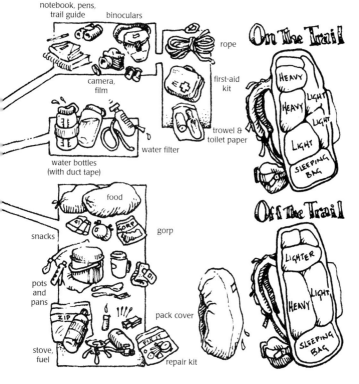

notebook, pens, trail guide
binoculars
rope
camera, film
first-aid kit
water bottles (with duct tape)
water filter
trowel & toilet paper

On The Trail
HEAVY
LIGHT
HEAVY
LIGHT
LIGHT
SLEEPING BAG

food
snacks
gorp
pots and pans
stove, fuel
pack cover
repair kit

Off The Trail
LIGHTER
LIGHT
HEAVY
SLEEPING BAG

PUTTING ON YOUR PACK

Putting on the pack is something you'll do many times a day, so minimize the energy used. For loads under 25 pounds (11 kg), you can simply swing the pack onto your back. For heavier loads, follow these steps:

1. Using both hands, pick up the pack by the shoulder straps with the harness system facing you.

2. Lift the pack onto one bent leg (we'll use the right leg in this example).

3. Twist your torso slightly, slip your right arm through the right shoulder strap.

4. Swing the pack onto your back.

5. Tighten the hipbelt fully by bending forward slightly and pulling in your stomach muscles as you cinch the belt. (The side tension straps on the belt should be slackened before you do this, then tightened once the belt is done up.)

stabilizer
straps

With very heavy loads (50 pounds/22 kg or more), bend toward the pack as you slip your arm through the shoulder strap and then carefully shift it onto your back. If you can find a boulder, tree stump, or bank to put the pack on when you take it off, you can simply back into the harness.

For most hiking you'll want to have the shoulder and stabilizer straps loose enough that most of the weight is on your hips. When the pack is properly adjusted you should just be able to slide a finger between your shoulder and the shoulder straps. The harness will probably need minor adjustments while you walk.

If the pack sways on steep descents or when crossing rough ground, bushwhacking, and scrambling, loosen the top stabilizer straps, tighten the shoulder straps, and then retighten the stabilizers. This will pull the pack in close to your body for maximum stability.

TRAIL ETIQUETTE

When hiking, leave as little sign of your passing as possible.

- Never intentionally disturb wildlife or other hikers.

- Stay on the trail—this includes not cutting corners or walking off the trail edge, even if trails are wet and muddy, since doing so can damage the trail and lead to wide, unsightly ruts.

- In descent, follow switchbacks and resist the temptation to go straight down, which can lead to erosion scars as water follows your new trail.

- Don't take shortcuts made by other hikers (indeed, if you have time, block shortcuts so others don't use them and increase the erosion).

- When going cross-country, don't build cairns, cut blazes, or leave other marks. These detract from the wilderness feel and may lead to a new trail forming.

- Walk in single file to avoid widening the trail.

- When you meet other hikers, a friendly greeting is fine, but keep it brief unless the others clearly want to talk. Solitude is important to many hikers. If there's danger or a problem ahead—you've just seen a bear, or a bridge has been washed out—by all means mention it. But don't offer advice regarding the trail or the terrain that lies ahead unless you're asked: it may detract from a sense of adventure or exploration.

- On narrow trails, step aside to allow other hikers to pass, including hikers going the same direction but moving faster than you.

- If you catch up with a slower party, wait for them to let you by.

- If you meet horses or other pack animals, step aside and let them pass, moving well off the trail if possible and staying still so you don't spook them.

- Bicyclists, on the other hand, should always give way to you, but they may be moving very fast and may not see you until the last moment. Stay alert for bicycles on trails where they are permitted.

BACKPACKING BASICS

Mono Lake, California

  BACKPACKING BASICS

DISTANCES AND TURNAROUND TIME

When planning a hike, it's easy to overestimate how far you can comfortably walk in a day. During a hike you will quickly determine more realistic distances.

If you find you can't manage the planned daily mileage, check the map or trail guide for a shorter route to your destination. Another option is to turn back earlier than planned to ensure you make it back to your starting point before you run out of food. Based on your actual mileage rate, estimate how far you can go and still return in the time available. If you have a pickup arranged for the finish, return to the start with enough time to notify them about your change of plan. You should in any case contact anyone expecting to hear from you as soon as possible after you get off the trail.

On long-distance hikes you may need to ration your food until you reach the next supply point and then take on more food for the next section.

Finally, learn from your experience: keep records of your mileage rates for each hike and use that information in future trip planning.

ON AND OFF THE TRAIL

HIKING ON A WELL MAINTAINED, WELL-MARKED TRAIL is relatively easy. The main skill is in finding a comfortable pace. Off-trail hiking is usually slower and more uncertain than trail hiking. Don't plan or expect to cover the same distance in the same time, and be prepared to alter your route if the terrain becomes difficult. Flexibility and an open mind are important assets when you leave the trails behind.

READING THE TERRAIN

When hiking off-trail the quickest and easiest way between two points is rarely a straight line. For ease of passage, go with the terrain, not against it. This means learning about the topography and the vegetation types so you can work out where the easiest hiking terrain is. Surveying the area from passes or summits can help find the easiest hiking routes, especially if you have binoculars. When searching for an easy route, consider the following:

- Are there grassy ridges along which you can stride to avoid a brush-choked valley?
- Is there a strip of bare ground or gravel beside the creek that will keep you out of the dense forest?
- Is there a shallow creek that you can walk along?
- Winding your way through open, mature forest or linking a series of meadows will be easier than clambering over the boulder- and talus-covered slopes above.
- Animal trails can be the easiest ways through forests—but avoid bear trails! (See page 46.)
- In deserts, dry washes frequently make for good hiking away from the spines and thorns of vegetation.

RHYTHM AND PACE

The easiest and most enjoyable way to hike is to establish a rhythm and pace that feels comfortable and can be sustained for long periods. Short bursts of rapid hiking interspersed with long rests while you get your breath back are more tiring than a slower, steady pace. If you can't talk comfortably, you're going too fast.

When hiking in a group, set the pace by the slowest member—otherwise, slower hikers will struggle to keep up and will soon become tired and demoralized. Stay at rest stops until the last person in has rested or eaten; if someone is tired and wants to camp early, do so. And if you're finding it hard to keep up with the group's pace, or you find the distance hiked each day too tiring, speak up! Struggling to keep up isn't fun and could be unsafe for you and the other members of the group.

Estimated Travel Speeds

Allow one hour for every 3 miles (5 km) and an additional 20 minutes for every 1,000 feet (300 m) of ascent.

TAKING BREAKS

How often you stop for a rest is a personal matter. Some hikers find that stopping at regular intervals and for a fixed time—say, five-minute stops every hour—is the best way to organize rests. In good weather scenic viewpoints make good rest stops. In storms seek out the shelter of the forest or a large boulder or rockface. If the storm is really bad, it could be worth erecting your tent or tarp. Otherwise, keep rest stops very short so you don't get cold.

For a stop to be restorative, you need to stay warm when it's cold and cool when it's hot, have something to eat and drink, and get off your feet. If the weather is cool, don an extra layer of clothing as soon as you stop—don't wait until you start to feel cold. It's easier to *stay* warm than to *get* warm. In the heat, find a shady spot. Use a rock or tree as a backrest or, failing that, prop up your pack on a hiking pole or stick and use it instead. Stretching out your legs is a good way to rest them. If they ache or feel swollen, elevating them on a rock or log can give great relief.

WEATHER

FORECASTING

With a little skill it's possible to make fairly good weather predictions at least some of the time. A barometer (see next page) can help with this.

First, always get the latest weather forecast before starting a hike. Take into account that forecast accuracy decreases the farther out it extends. A small weather radio could prove helpful for listening to forecasts in the backcountry. However, direct observations are more important than any forecast. Heed signs of an approaching storm even if the forecast is for fine weather.

Understanding cloud types is very useful for predicting the weather. Keep in mind that cloud types aren't always distinct and frequently merge into one another. In general, if clouds are thickening and advancing across the sky, it may rain or snow. If the wind increases, the storm is likely moving fast and will arrive sooner than if it's fairly calm.

Cirrus: Very high, fuzzy wisps, often in long curved threads (sometimes known as mare's tails). May indicate the leading edge of a storm system. If they thicken, rain may be on the way.

Cirrostratus: When cirrus thickens enough to cover most of the sky, it becomes cirrostratus. Often accompanied by a halo around the sun or moon. Rain or snow is likely.

Altostratus: Lower than cirrostratus, altostratus is thick enough to obscure the sun. Usually indicates rain or snow is on the way. The sky is gray, with little detail in the cloud.

Nimbostratus: Dark, ragged clouds that sometimes appear below the solid sheet of altostratus; often bring heavy rain.

Cumulus: The familiar white-cotton clouds; these generally accompany fine weather. Larger ones can produce showers.

Cumulonimbus: Thunderstorms are likely if cumulus clouds start to deepen and darken, towering into the sky and sometimes developing flat, anvil-shaped tops. If you see these clouds forming, descend from high, exposed places and stay away from flat, open areas.

  BACKPACKING BASICS

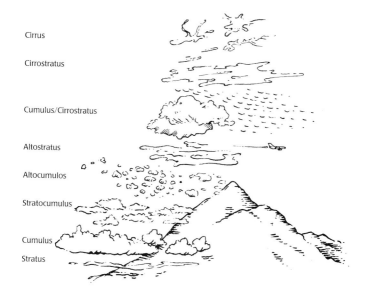

Cirrus

Cirrostratus

Cumulus/Cirrostratus

Altostratus

Altocumulos

Stratocumulus

Cumulus

Stratus

Stratocumulus: Cumulus clouds may also coalesce into a more solid sheet known either as stratocumulus (fairly low) or altocumulus (higher up). Showers are possible when these clouds are present.

A more sure way to predict the weather is with an altimeter-barometer, which records changes in air pressure. Most electronic barometers can be set to measure the change in pressure overnight (when hiking this can't be easily done unless you stay at the same elevation). If the pressure drops rapidly, a big storm with strong winds is likely within twenty-four hours. A slower drop means any wet weather will probably take longer to arrive. Conversely, a steady rise in barometric pressure means high pressure is building, which usually indicates dry, fine weather. No change means just that—the weather is stable. You can also predict the weather from altimeter readings, though you have to remember that an apparent rise in altitude means that pressure is falling. So, if your camp has risen several hundred feet during the night, the pressure will have dropped and a storm will be on the way. This is because barometric pressure drops with elevation, and this change is used to measure altitude. So when the pressure changes, the altimeter will give a different elevation even though it hasn't moved.

READING THE WIND

The direction and strength of the wind can affect how far and how easily you can walk. Keeping a check on the wind can help you with both weather forecasting and choosing your route.

What's Up?

Signs of Worsening Weather

Falling barometer (carry an altimeter to provide pressure readings)

Rapidly building cumulus clouds

Lenticular clouds and lowering clouds

Signs of Improving Weather

Rising barometer

Cloud breaks

Cloud bases rising

Signs of Continued Fair Weather

No clouds, steadily rising barometer

Barometer high and steady

Cumulus clouds

Dew or frost in the morning, with no fog

Morning fog that burns off rapidly

No afternoon clouds

Source: *Reading Weather*, Jim Woodmencey

BACKPACKING BASICS

When planning a route for a windy day, note that winds often funnel and pick up speed through passes, notches, and narrow valleys. These are not places to plan rest stops. In really strong winds, avoid them completely.

The wind speed often diminishes on the downwind side of a mountain but increases again when the wind streams rejoin.

The direction storms usually come from varies from area to area. Try to find out in advance the normal storm track for the area where you're hiking. Then, if the wind increases from that direction, you'll know that a storm is probably approaching. You can then decide to make camp early or to change your route.

Winds are most challenging above timberline, where they're stronger and there's little shelter. Narrow ridges and exposed cliff edges can be particularly dangerous in very strong winds. When the wind strengthens, especially if it does so quickly, it's a good idea to descend.

If you're caught in very strong winds far from any shelter, go with the wind rather than fight against it if possible, even if that means retracing your steps. Hiking into winds much over 30 mph (48 kph) can be very tiring.

LIGHTNING

If a thunderstorm is approaching or breaks around you, avoid summits, ridge crests, isolated trees, small stands of trees, lakeshores, open meadows, and shallow caves. You don't want to be or be near the highest object around. Seek out deep forests, the bases of high cliffs, large boulders, and depressions in flat areas.

Beware of ground currents. Don't lie or sit on the ground. Instead, crouch on an insulating mat, keeping your feet together. Put metal gear, such as framed packs and hiking poles, some distance away so they don't burn you if there's a nearby strike. Groups should spread out.

To determine how far away a storm is, count the seconds between a lightning flash and the following crack of thunder. Five seconds means the storm is a mile away; ten seconds means it's two miles away.

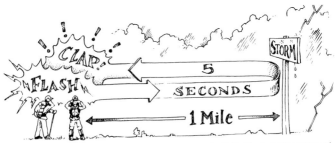

Time from seeing lightning strike to thunder in seconds, divided by 5, equals distance of storm from you in miles.

HAIL

If a thunderstorm is imminent, you might be in for hail, as well. Fortunately, hail falls in only a portion of the thunderstorm area, generally where updrafts and downdrafts are strong. If hail starts to fall, head for a lower elevation, if possible, and seek cover to avoid being pelted and possibly injured.

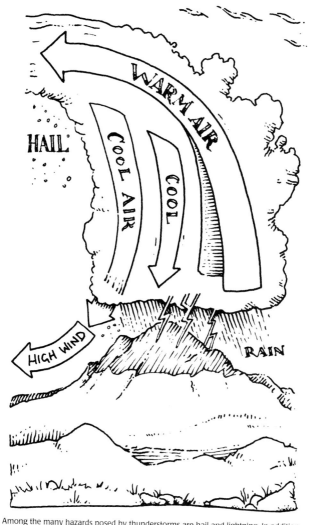

Among the many hazards posed by thunderstorms are hail and lightning. In addition, extremely strong wind gusts can pose a threat to climbers. If you sense the onset of a thunderstorm, seek low ground.

STAYING WARM

Adjust your clothing as needed to stay comfortably warm: not too hot or too cold.

- If you start feeling cold, don't continue hiking without adjusting your clothing or donning more items if necessary.

- In cool weather you are likely to leave a campsite or trailhead wearing a warm top and maybe hat and gloves. Once you start to warm up, stop and remove these items unless it is getting colder. Overheating leads to sweat-soaked clothes—even with modern synthetics—that will chill you when you stop.

- Putting on or taking off a hat makes a huge difference. You lose a massive amount of heat through an uncovered head, so donning a hat can warm you quickly.

- A windproof outer garment is imperative in cold winds. Keep windproof shells handy so you can quickly don them on breezy passes and summits. If you see clouds racing overhead or hear the wind roaring across a pass, put on your windproof clothing just before you get there so you don't lose any heat.

- Don a warm top as soon as you reach a rest stop. Don't wait until you start to feel cool. Again, it's much easier to stay warm than to get warm.

- Eating provides warmth. Have a snack when you stop to put on warm clothing.

- If you really can't get warm, don't push on; stop and make camp, get in your sleeping bag, and have a hot drink and a hot meal.

hat

windproof outer garment

gloves

BACKPACKING BASICS

wool hat

polypropylene undershirt

fleece top

hot beverage

wind- and water-proof outer layer

windpants

articulated knees

gaiters

socks

boots

Hats and gloves are easy to don and shed as needed.

STAYING DRY

Getting wet isn't in itself a problem—being wet and *cold* is. It's unpleasant and uncomfortable and can lead to hypothermia. So in temperatures where you need to wear more than shorts and a T-shirt to stay warm, stay as dry as possible.

- In calm weather or sheltered places (forests, canyons, below cliffs), consider using an umbrella to avoid the condensation problems often accompanying the use of rain garments. However, always carry rain clothing: umbrellas aren't easy to use in gusty or strong winds and may collapse. They are also awkward in forests with low-hanging branches and in dense brush.

- Put on your rain jacket as soon as the first drops fall. Don't wait to see if it will rain heavily. If it does and you get wet, you'll stay wet.

- In prolonged rain even the best waterproof-breathable rain clothing won't allow all the moisture vapor your body gives off to escape. To minimize condensation, open jacket vents, if you can do so without letting rain in.

- The neck is a key ventilation point, so put the hood up only when you must. A waterproof hat allows moist air to escape at the neck. A hood stops it.

- Being warm and damp is far preferable to being cold and wet. In heavy rain and strong winds, close your rain jacket even if it leads to dampness inside. In such conditions you may need rain pants, too.

- It's very easy to overheat and to start sweating in rain clothing. Often a thin base layer is all you need under a rain jacket while you are moving. Don't wear cotton, though: it absorbs masses of water, is very cold when damp, and takes ages to dry. If you're wearing

eating and drinking provides warmth

a cotton top and rain starts, change to a synthetic or wool top.

- You'll need a warmer layer as soon as you stop. Keep stops short, too, unless you find good shelter.

- Keep your water-sensitive gear (sleeping bag, spare clothing) in waterproof bags and put on your pack cover if you have one.

- Keep items you'll need along the way, like snacks, in a jacket pocket or the top pocket of your pack so you don't have to open the pack and risk getting the contents wet.

STAYING COOL

Hiking under a blazing sun can be exhausting, to say nothing of risking sunburn and dehydration. To keep reasonably cool you need shade, especially for your head.

umbrella for shade

hat with wide brim

shirt with UV protection

- Wear a hat with a broad brim or a peak and a Foreign Legion– style neck cloth. The best hat is loose fitting so you don't get too sweaty under it; a neck cord keeps it on in wind.

- To cool down, soak your hat in water whenever you pass a creek or pool. Or soak a bandanna and wrap it around your neck.

- You can also use a bandanna as a makeshift neck cloth tucked under a baseball cap.

- If the trail is roomy, an umbrella is a great way to create some shade, especially if you cover the outside with reflective silver material.

- In extreme heat, rest in the middle of the day and hike in the cooler hours of morning and evening. If you can't find a tree or rock to provide shade, put up a tarp or pitch your tent and sit in its shade (not inside, though, where it can get very hot).

- Sunglasses are useful in bright sunshine, especially if hiking over pale sand or rock.

DIFFICULT TERRAIN

ASCENDING STEEP TERRAIN

Uphill hiking requires shorter steps and a slower pace than hiking on level ground. A rhythmic chant, either aloud or under your breath, can help. Try counting, repeating a phrase ("I will reach the top, I will reach the top!"), singing a song, or reciting rhythmic verses.

When climbing slopes where there is no trail, it's much easier to make your own switchbacks than to try to climb straight up. Before starting up the ascent, try to pick out a route from below—binoculars are useful here—and look for large rocks or trees to use as landmarks as you climb. If you can't see all the way to the top, pick out your route in stages. Climb to your first landmark and then look ahead and plan the next section.

If you have to use your hands to clamber over boulders or up small rock faces, don't climb anything you couldn't descend if you're turned back by obstacles higher up.

a switchback route is an easier climb than the path straight up

keep weight over feet

short steps

stick downhill for extra support

short steps, sideways to hill on soft slopes

DESCENDING STEEP TERRAIN

Generally speaking, it's actually easier to climb up a steep slope than to climb down. In particular, descending steep slopes where there is no trail requires great care. Again, plan your route as far as possible before you start down. But keep in mind that small cliffs and drop-offs are likely to be invisible from above, so approach blind edges very cautiously. If the ground appears to be dropping away very steeply, traverse across the slope and look for a safer way down. Hiking poles or a staff can be used for support—if your poles are adjustable, lengthen them so you can place them well down the slope. That way you don't have to lean out from the slope as you descend.

As with ascending, short steps are best. Long ones can easily throw you out of balance. Keep your weight over your feet, too. It's tempting to lean into the slope because it feels safer, but you're more likely to slip.

Big packs can make descending steep rocky slopes difficult. If this is so, you can always lower your pack on the end of a length of rope (such as your bearbagging rope), and then climb down after it. Don't do this unless you're certain you can climb down, though.

keep weight over feet—don't lean back into slope

TALUS, SCREE, AND BOULDERS

Rocky terrain varies from small stones that move under your feet (scree) to larger rocks and small boulders (talus). As with other tricky terrain, you should pick out a route in advance—at least to the next large boulder. This leaves you free to concentrate on your balance and the next step, looking up occasionally to make sure you are going the right direction.

Before crossing a rocky area, tighten your harness straps so your pack hugs your back and doesn't lurch from side to side, throwing you off balance. A hiking pole or poles can help with balance, but be wary of catching the tip between two rocks. Keep your weight over your feet and take short steps, testing each rock for stability before you put your weight on it. When descending, don't lean back or take long strides—both are likely to lead to slips. When ascending or traversing, don't lean into the slope; this also leads to slips.

Since it's impossible to avoid slipping on the small, loose stones known as *scree*, it's best not to try but rather to let the stones run under your feet as you descend. Before descending a scree slope, look to see what lies below. If you can't see the bottom of the slope there may be a cliff there, and it would be safer to descend elsewhere. In descent, let the stones slide under your feet. To stay in balance, keep your knees bent and put your weight on your heels first. Don't go too fast, especially with a big load, so that if you do slip you won't hurt yourself.

Ascending scree is boring, exhausting, and slow. Avoid it if possible. If not, accept that it will take a long time and that you will slip back a little with almost every step. Kicking your toes into the stones can help, as can angling across the slope, but nothing will make it easy.

If you send a rock hurtling down the mountainside when hiking on scree or talus, yell "rock!" loudly if there might be anyone below you. And if you hear someone yell "rock," don't look up—crouch and put your arms over your head.

tighten pack straps

hiking pole for balance—watch getting the tip caught

keep knees bent

small boulders (talus) can make climbing difficult

FORDING RIVERS AND CREEKS

Fording flowing water that is greater than ankle deep can be dangerous, and you should avoid it whenever possible. If in doubt, *don't cross*—even if it means you can't complete your hike or if the added distance means you might run short of food. Going hungry is far better than drowning.

Shallow rivers or creeks can often be forded safely, however. Step from boulder to boulder, checking with each step that the boulder isn't going to roll when you put your weight on it. If there aren't any or enough boulders, you'll have to wade. Unless you can see the bottom clearly and it's sand, mud, or gravel, don't cross in bare feet. To protect your feet, wear your spare footwear or, if they're already wet, your boots.

If the water looks too deep or strong to ford safely, look up- and downstream for an easier crossing point. Check the map for any wide or braided areas. (Several shallow channels are easier to cross than one deep one, and wide areas are usually shallower than narrow ones.) If the map shows rapids or waterfalls downstream, cross below them so you don't risk being swept over.

Climbing to a high bank or hillside may give an overview of the river and enable you to identify a likely ford. Look for straight sections of water, since banks are often undercut, and the water deeper, at bends in the river. Avoid whitewater, and look for shingle banks, small islets, and large boulders that you can use as safe rest points. Stay away from half-submerged trees, though—getting tangled up in these can be dangerous.

It is possible to cross rivers on log-jams or fallen trees, but check the logs carefully to make sure they don't roll. If in doubt, retreat. Straddling the log is safer than trying to walk across.

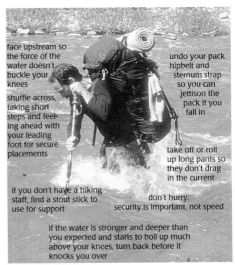

face upstream so the force of the water doesn't buckle your knees

shuffle across, taking short steps and feeling ahead with your leading foot for secure placements

undo your pack hipbelt and sternum strap so you can jettison the pack if you fall in

take off or roll up long pants so they don't drag in the current

if you don't have a hiking staff, find a stout stick to use for support

don't hurry: security is important, not speed

if the water is stronger and deeper than you expected and starts to boil up much above your knees, turn back before it knocks you over

If the stream is glacier- or snowmelt-fed or full of rain runoff from a recent storm, it could be worth waiting for the level to go down. Glaciers and snow often freeze overnight, leading to a much-reduced flow early in the morning. Streams that rise rapidly in heavy rain can fall just as quickly soon after the rain stops.

Members of a group can cross by holding onto each other's waists, the first person facing upstream and using a staff in her free hand. Or, three people can form a triangle, with their arms around the others' shoulders, and shuffle across. Do not use a rope: it can trap a person under water if they are swept away.

If you feel cold after a ford, eat some high-carbohydrate snacks, don warm clothing, and start hiking fast.

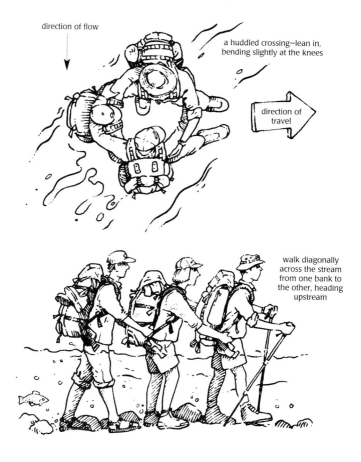

direction of flow

a huddled crossing—lean in, bending slightly at the knees

direction of travel

walk diagonally across the stream from one bank to the other, heading upstream

BUSHWHACKING

At times you may have to force your way through dense vegetation. There is no easy way to do this. Forget about trying to maintain a straight line for even short distances when bushwhacking. Instead, take the easiest line, zigzagging as much as necessary. Exploit any gaps in the bush, such as meadows, creek banks, dry washes, and lakeshores, even if they aren't on your line of travel. There may be easier ground on the far side. Don't expect to make much progress, either. A mile an hour is a respectable speed; half a mile an hour may be hard to achieve. And while bushwhacking don't forget to check the map and compass occasionally to ensure you're still going in the right direction—it's easy to become completely disoriented.

In some areas the problem may be a tangle of fallen trees rather than dense bushes. In the worst places it's both! When climbing over downed trees, watch out for branches springing up as you step on them. If you can, go around the tangle rather than over it.

gear outside the pack may be torn or damaged—this would be better in the pack or under the lid

keep an eye out for good routes and try to keep out of vegetation above head height

long sleeves and long pants protect against scratches

SNOW

Early and late in the season, snow may obscure sections of trail. On flat terrain make sure you can locate the trail on the other side of the snow. This may mean working along the edge of the snow until you find the trail. Here are some other tips for traveling in snow:

- If you're not carrying an ice ax or crampons, venture onto snow slopes only if the snow is fairly soft.

- Hiking poles or a staff can help with balance, but they won't easily stop a slide. Kick the edges of your boots into the snow to make platforms, and don't hurry.

- Check out what lies below the snow slope. If there's a drop-off and the slope is steep, you should find another route, perhaps climbing above the snow.

Deep, soft snow is hard to cross on foot. You have to lift each leg high and then push it back into the snow, a tiring procedure known as post-holing. Poles can help you keep your balance, but it's still a slow and difficult process. If you can go around a large soft snowfield, do so even if it makes your trip much longer.

Descend soft snow using the plunge step: head straight down, ramming your heels into the snow and keeping your weight over them. Make sure there is a safe runout below the slope in case you slip.

ice ax: this should be in your hand, not on your pack

crampons worn for hard snow

ice ax on uphill side for security

ENCOUNTERS WITH WILDLIFE

KEEP YOUR DISTANCE

For the most part, seeing wildlife is one of the joys of hiking and not a problem. However, for both your safety and that of

the animals, there are a few basic guidelines to follow—all of which boil down to "do not disturb." When you encounter animals, observe them from a distance rather than seeing how near you can get. If they seem agitated, move away. Few animals are likely to attack, but some will if they feel cornered, particularly if they have young to defend.

Do not feed any animals you encounter, as the food isn't good for them and it may encourage them to hassle future hikers or raid their packs. Don't leave food scraps at rest stops, either. For information on animal-proofing your campsite, see pages 91–95.

SNAKES AND SCORPIONS

When hiking in rattlesnake or scorpion country, be wary around bushes and rock piles and don't put your hands behind logs or rocks or anywhere you can't see. If walking in sandals or low-cut shoes, whether on the trail or around camp, be especially careful to stay on open ground. (For first aid for snakebites, see page 128.)

high socks and boots are good protection from snakes and scorpions

don't place your hands behind rocks

FLYING INSECTS AND TICKS

Mosquitoes, no-see-ums, blackflies—these tiny creatures can turn an otherwise-perfect hike into a nightmare! Ward off biting insects by using insect repellent on bare skin and clothing, especially cuffs and collars, and wearing tightly woven clothing and head nets. Hiking briskly works, too, as most insects can't fly very fast. Rest in breezy places and away from standing water—wind keeps some biting insects from flying, and water is where they breed.

Ticks are harder to avoid and more of a long-term threat, since their bites can lead to serious illnesses. Ticks are usually at their worst in spring and early summer and often infest grassy areas. They hang on the tips of grass stems waiting for a passing victim, which means that they usually attach themselves to your legs first. Ticks have eight legs and look a little like tiny, flat spiders. In tick season and tick country, check your clothes and body for them at rest stops and in camp.

If you think you might be the victim of a tick bite, see the information on tick first aid, page 129.

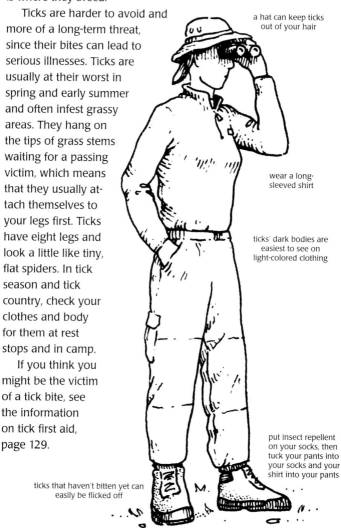

a hat can keep ticks out of your hair

wear a long-sleeved shirt

ticks' dark bodies are easiest to see on light-colored clothing

put insect repellent on your socks, then tuck your pants into your socks and your shirt into your pants

ticks that haven't bitten yet can easily be flicked off

BEARS

When hiking in bear country—especially grizzly bear country—it is best for you and for the bears if you avoid meeting each other. The first precaution is to ask local rangers and land managers about recent bear activity in the area. Are there any areas where they have been problems and that you should stay away from?

On the trail try to ensure that any bears will know you are there long before you are close enough to be seen as a threat. If the wind is behind you they'll smell you coming, and if it's fairly quiet they'll probably hear you, as well. However, if the wind is in your face and there's a noisy creek beside the trail or you're hiking in dense vegetation, a bear might not realize you are there until you are very close. In these situations making a noise is a good idea. Shouting, singing, clapping, and ringing a loud bell will alert bears to your presence (tinkling those little "bear bells" won't). When going cross-country, avoid bear trails—which often have two lanes or separate depressions where the bears tread—especially in dense brush or forest and near berry patches and creek sides.

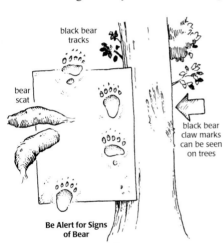

black bear tracks

bear scat

black bear claw marks can be seen on trees

Be Alert for Signs of Bear

Watch out for bear sign, too—piles of scat, paw prints, scratches on tree trunks, dug-over patches of earth. If these appear fresh, be very wary and don't remain in the area or camp anywhere nearby.

In open country, scan the distant area, with binoculars if you have them. Bears are big, and you can often see them quite a distance away. Is that a tree stump, a rock, or a grizzly? If you see a bear make a very wide detour around it.

Bears are attracted by certain smells, especially food and scented soaps and deodorants. Unscented soaps and foods with little smell are best. Keep food well wrapped in the pack,

BACKPACKING BASICS

too. If you spill food on your clothes, wash them out as soon as possible. Do not sleep in clothes you wore while cooking. (For more on animal-proofing your camp kitchen, see pages 91–95.)

If you carry bear-repellent spray when in bear territory, keep it handy on your pack hipbelt or somewhere you can grab it fast. It's only a last resort, though, and not a reason to take risks. These sprays don't hurt the animal, but they're unpleasant enough that they may drive it away, at least long enough for you to depart, as well.

What do you do if you meet an aggressive bear? Advice is mixed, but many experts agree on the following:

- Don't run. If the bear chases you, you won't be able to outrun it. Instead, according to most experts, it's best to stand your ground and try to make yourself appear as big and imposing as possible (this is easier if there is more than one of you). However, don't look directly at the bear or act aggressively.

- Make calming noises and slowly back away.

- For black bears: If the bear charges and follows through (most charges are bluffs) fight back. Otherwise the bear may start to eat you.

- For grizzlies: Lie down and play dead with your hands clasped behind your neck. Don't move until you're sure the bear has gone, then leave slowly. Most grizzly attacks happen because the bear sees the victim as a threat. Once the threat appears to be over, the bear is likely to wander away.

possible position for playing dead

- In grizzly country it's best to sleep in a tent rather than in the open, as bears usually avoid tents (unless they smell food).

- Finally, remember that an encounter with a bear is very unlikely and being attacked by one extremely improbable. Take the necessary precautions but don't let the knowledge that bears are out there spoil your hike.

Where Are We?

NAVIGATION

KEEPING TRACK ON THE MAP

Always keep your map or trail guide easily accessible so you can consult them whenever you need to. If they are buried in your pack you might guess the way rather than dig them out—that's a good way to get lost! If you'll need the map frequently, carry it in a garment pocket so you can reach it without having to take off your pack. If you're on a well-marked trail or familiar terrain, a pack pocket should be fine.

Before you set out for the day, go over your planned route on the map or in the trail guide. You'll know what to expect, how far you have to walk to the next water supply, and how far it is to your next planned camp.

As you hike, keep an eye on the map and route even when you're in a group. The others might not be doing so! And if you think the leader has gone astray, say so.

When following a clear trail, an occasional map or trail guide check should be enough to show you where you are and how far you have to go. This is best done at points where there is an easily identifiable landmark, such as a lake or large cliff, or in open areas where you can see the surrounding country and relate it to the map. To make this easier, orient the map (see illustration opposite, top): set the compass on the map with north aligned with the top of the map (1); then turn the map until the magnetic compass needle also points north (2). Features on the ground should now be easy to identify on the map. Put a straight edge, such as the side of the compass, on the map so it points to the feature on the ground (3); the feature on the map should lie along the line of the straight edge.

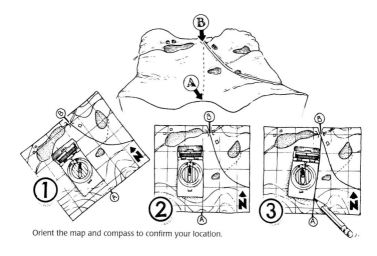

Orient the map and compass to confirm your location.

If you want to know exactly where you are and you can identify several features on the ground, draw lines from them on the
map. Where they cross is where you are (see illustration below).

Popular trails are usually clear on the ground and often
marked by blazes on trees, piles of stones (cairns or ducks),
posts marked with the trail symbol or other signs. As long as
the trail is distinct and there is an occasional marker, you
should have no problem following the trail. Watch out for
junctions, though, especially unmarked ones. If the trail starts
to fade away and you don't see any markers, you might have
strayed onto a side trail or animal path. To check whether
you're on the right trail, retrace your steps either to the junc-

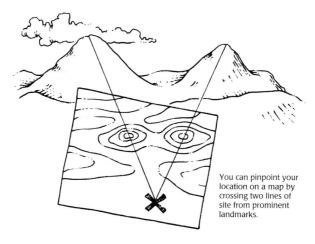

You can pinpoint your
location on a map by
crossing two lines of
site from prominent
landmarks.

tion you missed or the last trail marker. If a junction is un-marked, check your map or trail guide rather than guessing which branch to take. The most obvious choice may not be the right one.

Sometimes a junction may not even be marked on the map or described in the trail guide. Trails are sometimes relocated, and maps and guides are often out of date. If this is the case, you need to use your compass and map and determine which direction the trail you want should go. If the trail isn't marked on the map, take a map bearing on a prominent landmark the trail passes, such as a lake or cliff, and follow the trail that runs in that direction. Based on the distance and your current mileage rate, estimate how long it should take to reach that feature. When you arrive you'll know you're still on the right trail. If the feature doesn't appear when you expect it to, don't push on too far hoping it will; instead, return to the junction and take another trail.

I always turn around every so often and look back the way I have come to see what the landscape looks like behind me. It will then look more familiar if I have to retrace my steps.

TAKING BEARINGS

On most trails you don't need a compass. (Always carry one as a backup, though.) However, when hiking cross-country or on little-used or unmaintained trails, a compass may be essential. At these times, keep your compass handy in a garment pocket or hanging around your neck.

With a compass you can take a bearing and find out which direction to walk to reach your destination. You can even do this in dense forest or thick mist as long as you know where you are on the map. A bearing is the angle between north and the direction you want to go. If you can see your destination but know that it won't be visible all the time, you can simply point the compass's direction-of-travel arrow at the spot and then turn the compass housing until the north end of the magnetic needle is aligned with the orienting arrow. As long as these two arrows are in line, following the direction-of-travel arrow will take you to your destination.

However, because it's hard to maintain even a remotely straight line over a long distance, it is best to take each bearing on a much closer feature (known as a checkpoint), walk to

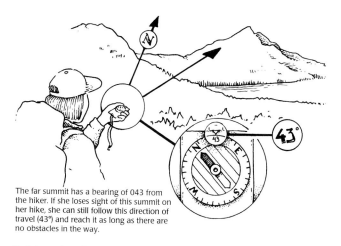

The far summit has a bearing of 043 from the hiker. If she loses sight of this summit on her hike, she can still follow this direction of travel (43°) and reach it as long as there are no obstacles in the way.

it, take a bearing on another feature, and so on. In featureless terrain, thick forest, or poor visibility you can use a companion as a checkpoint. Have her walk ahead until almost out of sight and then move to the side until in line with the bearing. Walk to her and repeat the process. It's slow but accurate.

When you are unsure which is the way to your destination, take a bearing off the map (see illustration below). Place the edge of the compass baseplate on the map on your current location. Then line up the edge with your destination (1). Next, rotate the compass housing so that the orienting arrow is aligned with north on the map (2 and 3). Take the compass off

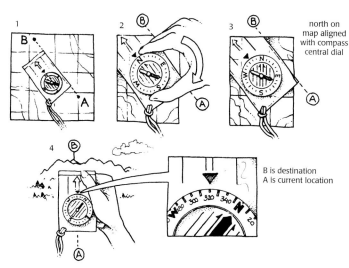

1

2

3

north on map aligned with compass central dial

4

B is destination
A is current location

the map and turn it until the orienting arrow and magnetic needle are aligned. The direction-of-travel arrow now points toward your destination (4). Read the number on the compass. This is your bearing. It's worth writing down—a compass housing can shift when you put it in a pocket.

In most areas you will also have to take into account the magnetic variation, or declination. This is the angle of difference between north on the map and the magnetic north the compass points to (which lies in the far north of Canada). North on the map may lie east or west of magnetic north. Magnetic north moves too, so the declination varies from year to year. Topo maps usually give the declination but may not list the rate of change. Once you know the area's declination, add or subtract it from your map bearing. If magnetic north is west of map north, add the difference. If magnetic north lies east of map north, subtract it. Topo maps have diagrams showing the angle and whether it is east or west of map north.

For example, on the Sabino Canyon quadrangle, which covers part of the Pusch Ridge Wilderness in Arizona, magnetic north is shown as 11.5 degrees east of true or map north.

The problem with taking a direct bearing on a destination you can't see is that if you're only slightly inaccurate, you could miss it. If there's a linear feature such as a creek, line of cliffs, canyon, or cross-trail near your destination, take a bearing on it to one side of the destination. That way when you get to the feature you'll know in which direction your destination lies.

GPS

A GPS (global positioning system) receiver is a great help to navigation, particularly in featureless or snow-covered terrain or when going cross-country through forest. With a GPS you can pinpoint exactly where you are. Put in the coordinates of your destination, and the receiver will give you the compass bearing (it calculates your position as it relates to the position of several satellites). You can walk with the receiver in hand, following the direction arrow, but it's easier to transfer the bearing to a compass and follow that, perhaps using the GPS again when you near your destination if you can't see it. This way you save batteries and don't risk losing the signal in dense forest or below high cliffs.

If you plot in the coordinates for your whole route in advance, you can just use the GPS without reference to map or compass. A GPS will also plot your route so you can retrace it if necessary.

You can download maps and map information to some GPS units. With one of these models you could have all the navigation information you need stored in your GPS. (Of course, you should still carry a map and compass.)

THE SUN AS COMPASS AND WATCH

The sun, in conjunction with an analog watch, can be used to find north or south. You can also use the sun to estimate roughly how long it will be until sunset, if you are trying to gauge the amount of available daylight before you need to find a night's campsite.

Telling Direction with Your Watch

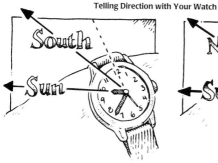 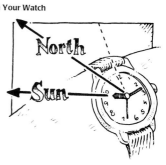

in the Northern Hemisphere, if you point your watch's hour hand at the sun, south will be located along the line midway between the hour hand and 12 o'clock

in the Southern Hemisphere, if you point your watch's hour hand at the sun, north will be located along the line midway between the hour hand and 12 o'clock

Estimating Time Until Sunset

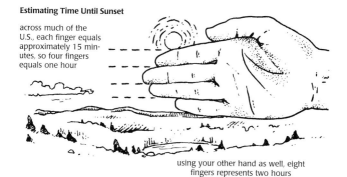

across much of the U.S., each finger equals approximately 15 minutes, so four fingers equals one hour

using your other hand as well, eight fingers represents two hours

WHEN YOU'RE LOST

WHAT TO DO

If you become unsure of your whereabouts, stay calm. Panic will only make matters worse. Stop, sit down, and think about where you might have gone astray. Check the map. Can you identify any features that might be visible on the ground and determine where you are?

If you can't work out where you are from the map, can you retrace your steps to a point you recognize or can identify on the map? If that's not possible, use your map and compass to work out the general direction of your destination. You can't be that far off your route. How long ago is it since you knew where you were?—that'll tell you how far you might have strayed. Once you know which direction to go, head that way and look for identifiable features and trails. If you come across any hazards, such as high cliffs, deep canyons, or a big river or lake, you should be able to find these on the map.

SIGNALING AIDS

If you can't find anywhere you can recognize or identify on the map and you don't know which way to walk, you may have to wait for help. The person you left your itinerary with should call out a search when you don't return, but that could be a few days or even a week away, so you should signal for help.

A cell phone may solve your problem immediately, if it works—you may not get a signal in remote areas or in deep canyons and dense forests. Climbing higher, if it's safe to do so, might solve this. Don't rely on a cell phone, though.

Traditional methods of signaling for help use sound, light, and smoke:

- If you think other people might be nearby, try calling out.

- A whistle will carry farther than your voice, and you'll be able to keep signaling for longer. Six blasts, pause, six blasts is the international distress signal.

- Use your flashlight if you're somewhere it will be visible for a distance. Signal with six flashes, pause, six flashes.

- A fire can quickly attract attention, particularly in remote areas where searches are likely to be carried out by air—but light a fire only if conditions are not dangerously dry. Ideally, you should arrange three fires in a triangle, the international distress signal. Making lots of smoke is probably more important than the shape, though. To do this, put damp and green vegetation on a fire.

- For another way to attract aircraft, spread light- or bright-colored gear on the ground or reflect sunlight at the pilot with something bright and shiny such as a mirror, foil windscreen, watch face, or camera lens (see illustration).

- Flares will be seen from the air; they're worth carrying in remote places such as Alaska.

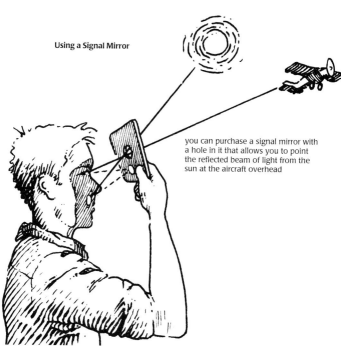

Using a Signal Mirror

you can purchase a signal mirror with a hole in it that allows you to point the reflected beam of light from the sun at the aircraft overhead

If the angle between the plane (or any target) and the sun is not too large (less than 90°), you can hold the mirror three to six inches away from your face and sight at the plane through the small hole in the center. The light from the sun will form a spot on your face and this spot will be reflected in the rear surface of the mirror. Then, still sighting on the target through the hole, adjust the angle of the mirror until the reflection of the light spot coincides with the hole in the mirror and disappears. The reflected light will then be accurately aimed at the target.

EMERGENCY SHELTER

If you get lost when away from camp on a side trip (or perhaps if a big storm comes in), you may have to take shelter for the night.

First, look for natural shelter—close to the trunk of a big tree, below an overhanging boulder, in a cave, in a dense thicket of small trees, anywhere that gives protection against the worst of the weather. (It is possible to build quite sophisticated shelters from natural materials, but this requires practice and is beyond the scope of this book. Just leaning branches against a tree or boulder and heaping foliage over them makes an effective, impromptu lean-to.)

The base of an overturned tree can make a protected shelter as can . . .

Fallen branches and sticks against a tree, or . . .

If you're likely to be immobile for a while and it's cold, don all your spare clothing, including rain gear. Sit hunched up, which retains more heat than lying down; if you're in a group, huddle close together.

If you regularly take hikes away from a base camp, it's worth carrying a lightweight bivouac bag or a small tarp in case of emergency (and also to use at cold rest stops). A small piece of closed-cell foam is useful, too, to sit on for insulation. Otherwise, sit on your pack. On any day trip I always like to feel I have the means to survive an unintended night out, if necessary.

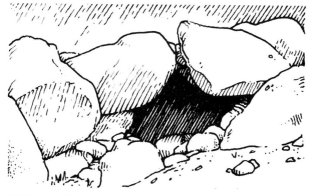

. . . a cave or grouping of rocks.

. . . A long fallen tree can also provide shelter.

Campcraft

SETTING UP CAMP

CHOOSING A CAMPSITE

The ideal campsite is soft, flat, and dry, sheltered from bad weather, not far from water, away from other campers, and has a superb view. Such campsites are not that easy to come by.

In some areas potential campsites are common. All you need is to know where the nearest water is. Mostly, though, it's wise to start looking for a site well before dark. If you pass a good one late in the afternoon, consider whether another is

likely to appear before sundown. What is the terrain like ahead? You don't want to start a long ascent or descent late in the day.

If a site hasn't presented itself toward the end of the day, you will need to search for one. Trail guides often list popular campsites and may suggest good places to camp. (However, if you can, try to camp away from others unless permit requirements restrict you to a certain site. Even if you don't want solitude, other campers might.)

Here are some pointers for finding a campsite:

- Check the map for a flat area (one with widely spaced contour lines) with water not too far away.

- When you reach the flat area, take off your pack and explore the area, looking for a good spot.

- Once you find a suitable spot, lie down on it to see if it's really level and comfortable. Remember, you only need enough flat ground to lie on. Bumps elsewhere don't matter.

- Soft ground is more comfortable than hard as long as it's not damp. Pine needles make an excellent bed.

- If possible, pitch your tent facing east. It's wonderful to wake up as the first rays of the sun strike you, and it warms you up quickly after a chilly night. *(continued)*

slightly sloping ground allows for better rain runoff

tent on dry ground, far from freshwater source to prevent contamination

- Cold air sinks into valley bottoms at night, so camping on a shelf higher up will make for a warmer camp.

- In rainy weather don't camp in a hollow or the lowest point of a flat area. You could wake up in a pool of water.

- In desert areas be cautious about camping in dry washes or the bottoms of canyons in case of flash floods.

- In forests make sure there are no dead trees or limbs that could fall on your tent.

- In areas where thunderstorms are common, camping above timberline or in the middle of a large open area may be unwise.

- If it's windy, seek a sheltered site in trees, behind a large boulder or cliff, or in the lee of a slope.

- The wind can whistle through passes, so avoid camping there unless it's quite calm.

- A bit of a breeze (but not a gale!) helps keep bugs away.

- In calm weather high-level campsites above timberline can be very appealing. It's best to work out an escape route, though, in case a storm blows in.

- Strong winds can keep you awake all night and can damage your tent, so shelter from wind is even more important than finding a flat site.

Lake St. Mary, Glacier National Park, Canada

There are three sorts of campsites: well used, occasionally used, and pristine. The first are characterized by hard bare ground and often also have fire rings, no fallen wood, and trails leading off to water sources and toilet sites. Animals may be a problem if they've become used to finding food at these sites. You should either use such sites (as required in some areas) or else camp a long way from them. Don't camp near an established site, as this is likely to spread the damage.

Avoid sites that haven't had much use. This will allow them to recover—or at least keep them from deteriorating further. Move on and search out somewhere no one has camped before.

When you use a pristine site, ensure that it still looks pristine when you leave. Look for a durable ground surface such as rock, bare ground, sand and gravel, pine needles, or dry vegetation such as grass. (If you can walk on the vegetation without leaving much of a mark, then it should survive camping.) Avoid damp ground, flowers, shrubs, and any soft, easily crushed vegetation. Don't move anything or alter the site in any way. If you have to shift a rock or piece of wood, when you leave put it back where you found it.

Unless there's no other option, always camp at least 100 feet (30 m) from water—this is a requirement in many areas. Lakeshores and riverbanks are often fragile, and you could disturb wildlife if you camp too near the water.

SETTING UP A TENT OR TARP

Pitching a shelter is easy as long as you have practiced well beforehand. If it's raining or windy you'll want to get your shelter up as quickly as possible. In wind stake down one corner of the shelter before you attach the poles so it can't blow away. For maximum stability pitch a tent with the rear into the wind. Once the tent or tarp is up, make sure all stakes are firmly in the ground and angled away from the shelter. Stake out all guylines and tighten them. If the stakes won't go into the ground, tie the guylines to rocks or trees. Extend stake points along the edge of the tent with lengths of cord if necessary.

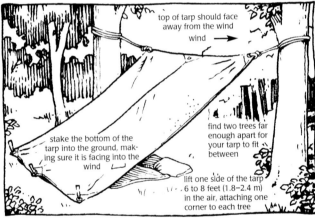

top of tarp should face away from the wind

wind ➝

find two trees far enough apart for your tarp to fit between

stake the bottom of the tarp into the ground, making sure it is facing into the wind

lift one side of the tarp 6 to 8 feet (1.8–2.4 m) in the air, attaching one corner to each tree

Lean-to Tarp

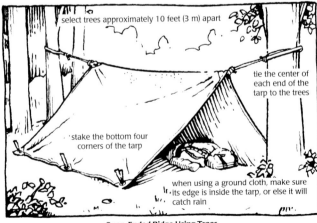

select trees approximately 10 feet (3 m) apart

tie the center of each end of the tarp to the trees

stake the bottom four corners of the tarp

when using a ground cloth, make sure its edge is inside the tarp, or else it will catch rain

Open-Ended Ridge Using Trees

  CAMPCRAFT

In rain you'll want to pitch the tent as fast as you can, especially if, like in most models, the inner tent goes up first and the rainfly is thrown over the top. To help keep the tent dry stake it out then spread the fly sheet over it. Next attach the poles and raise the tent with the fly spread over it.

If using a tarp for shelter, you have to decide what shape it is going to be. On sheltered sites a lean-to or open-ended ridge is fine. If it's windy or very wet, a low pyramid is more stable and protective. In heavy rain you want the lower edge of the tarp staked out at ground level, too. Otherwise, having the edge raised a little allows good airflow and reduces condensation. To support the tarp, use hiking poles or strong sticks; at-

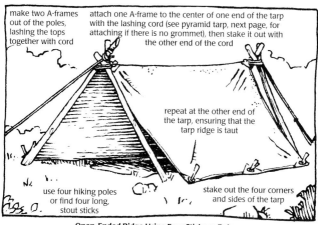

make two A-frames out of the poles, lashing the tops together with cord

attach one A-frame to the center of one end of the tarp with the lashing cord (see pyramid tarp, next page, for attaching if there is no grommet), then stake it out with the other end of the cord

repeat at the other end of the tarp, ensuring that the tarp ridge is taut

use four hiking poles or find four long, stout sticks

stake out the four corners and sides of the tarp

Open-Ended Ridge Using Four Sticks or Poles

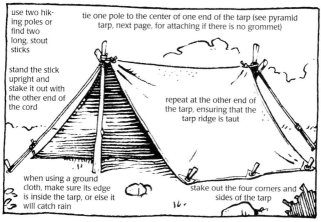

use two hiking poles or find two long, stout sticks

tie one pole to the center of one end of the tarp (see pyramid tarp, next page, for attaching if there is no grommet)

stand the stick upright and stake it out with the other end of the cord

repeat at the other end of the tarp, ensuring that the tarp ridge is taut

when using a ground cloth, make sure its edge is inside the tarp, or else it will catch rain

stake out the four corners and sides of the tarp

Open-Ended Ridge Using Two Sticks or Poles

tach guylines to them so you can pull the tarp taut. Instead of using poles, a tarp can be hung between two trees. Be flexible when pitching a tarp and think how you can fit it into the surroundings. Attachment points can be to the side or above the tarp, and you can use a pole in one corner if there isn't a tree or branch close enough. If there isn't a grommet where you want to attach a line, simply wrap a pebble in the fabric and tie off the "neck" with a piece of rope; then attach the line.

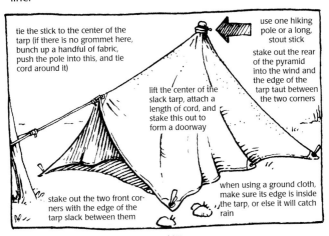

tie the stick to the center of the tarp (if there is no grommet here, bunch up a handful of fabric, push the pole into this, and tie cord around it)

use one hiking pole or a long, stout stick

stake out the rear of the pyramid into the wind and the edge of the tarp taut between the two corners

lift the center of the slack tarp, attach a length of cord, and stake this out to form a doorway

stake out the two front corners with the edge of the tarp slack between them

when using a ground cloth, make sure its edge is inside the tarp, or else it will catch rain

Pyramid Tarp

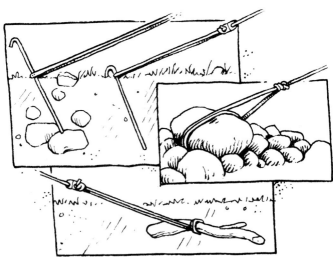

Top: Drive stake into ground at 45°, buried to the head if possible; if not, guyline should tie around the stake at ground level. Middle and Bottom: Two ways to tie down tarp lines without stakes.

CAMPCRAFT

CONDENSATION

In calm, humid conditions, condensation is unavoidable in both tents and tarps. Good ventilation minimizes condensation. Keep the following in mind:

- Don't close the tent doors unless you have to because of rain.

- Leave tent vents open.

- If you have to close the fly sheet doors, leave the top of the zippers open so warm, moist air can escape.

- Unless it's very windy, you can use hiking poles or sticks to hold up the tent doors, creating an awning and allowing plenty of air circulation.

- Keep wet gear outside the tent (if you have to bring it in, store it in the porch).

- Cook outside if you can, or leave tent doors open while cooking in the porch so steam can escape.

When condensation does occur, avoid touching the damp walls and make sure that your sleeping bag isn't in contact with them. In a two-skin tent ensure there is a good gap between the inner and outer and that you don't push the two together. In really wet weather you may have to seal up the tent and accept that there will be a lot of condensation come dawn.

In cold weather it's tempting to close all the doors and vents to keep the tent as warm as possible. This can result in copious condensation that then freezes and falls on you like snow in the morning. Leaving vents open even in extreme cold avoids this.

KNOTS TO KNOW

A few knots are useful for pitching tarps and when adding extra guylines to tents or replacing broken or lost guyline fasteners.

Tautline hitch: Doesn't slip when under tension but can be adjusted when slack. Use this instead of mechanical fasteners on guylines.

Overhand on the bight (left): Can be used to attach a guyline to an attachment point on a tent or tarp. Overhand knots can be hard to untie, however. If you'll want to untie the knot, use a rewoven figure eight (figure eight on a bight) (right).

Fisherman's knot: Use this to tie two ropes of equal diameter together, as when extending a guyline.

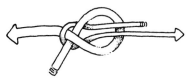

Sheet bend: Use this to join two lines of different thickness or to attach a guyline to the corner of a tarp where there is no attachment point.

Square or reef knot: Another choice for tying two lines of equal diameter together. It is very easy to untie. Be careful: tied incorrectly, this becomes a granny knot, which can slip.

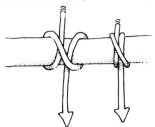

Clove hitch: Use this to tie a line to a tree to support a tarp.

  CAMPCRAFT

THE CAMPSITE BATHROOM

On some popular campsites, outhouses are provided. You should always use these when they're available. Usually, however, you'll need to find a suitable place yourself. Situate a toilet at least 200 feet (60 m) from any water source and from trails and anywhere people are likely to come across it. Given the option, choose a spot with a view but out of sight of trails or campsites. Dig a shallow cathole with your toilet trowel— 6 inches (15 cm) deep or so is enough. When you have finished your business, use a stick to mix the waste in with the soil and then fill in the hole. Cover it with leaves or debris to hide it.

Do not bury toilet paper with the waste—animals will just dig it up. Instead, double-bag the paper in plastic bags and carry it out. To do this cleanly, put your hand in a plastic bag, pick up the toilet paper, and pull the bag off your hand inside out with the toilet paper inside; then put it inside a larger bag. (Since you need to wash your hands, anyway, you can also just pick up the paper!) Burn toilet paper in a campfire if you have one. Don't burn it anywhere it could start a fire, however—forests have been destroyed due to this.

Here is more sanitation advice:

- For a natural alternative to toilet paper, use sand, pebbles, dead leaves, bark, grasses, or snow. Bury any of these in your cathole.

- Always carry out used sanitary protection or burn it on a hot campfire.

- After going to the toilet wash your hands thoroughly so you don't transfer any pathogens to food or cooking and drinking utensils.

- Do not urinate on vegetation, as animals may lick off the salts left behind and damage the plants.

BREAKING CAMP

In dry weather striking camp is easy. Unless you need to leave immediately, don't take down your tent or tarp until any condensation has dried. Unzip your sleeping bag and drape it over a dry boulder or branch so it can air. Air the bottoms of your sleeping pad and ground cloth too if these are damp.

In rain pack everything except your shelter under cover, making sure that water sensitive items are in waterproof bags. If it's really wet, strap your tarp or tent to the outside of your pack so it doesn't soak the contents. To keep the inner tent as dry as possible collapse the fly sheet on top of it, withdraw the poles, and pack the inner tent in its stuff sack under the fly sheet. When it's windy as well, leave one side of the fly sheet staked out until you're ready to pack it so it doesn't blow away. In strong winds

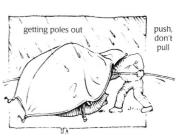

getting poles out

push, don't pull

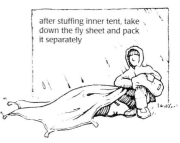

after stuffing inner tent, take down the fly sheet and pack it separately

collapse the fly sheet and tent before removing the poles to avoid damage.

Here are a few more hints for breaking camp:

- If you have sleeved tent poles, always push the poles out of the sleeves. If you pull them out they will probably come apart in the sleeves, which can make extracting them difficult.

- Wipe muddy stakes clean before packing.

- After striking camp and packing up all your gear, don't immediately swing your pack on your back and stride off. Take one last look around for anything you might have left. Did you fetch that pair of socks hung on a bush to dry? Are there any tent stakes still lying on the ground? How about trash, including bits of food wrappers?

- On a pristine site, once you're sure there's nothing else to pack, roughen up the ground where you slept so there's little sign you've been there.

CAMPSITE CHALLENGES

DARKNESS

If you have to make camp in the dark you may have to put up with a less-than-perfect site. Anywhere fairly flat and big enough will do. Don't put anything on the ground when un-packing—you could easily lose it in the dark. Put gear you need in the shelter; leave other stuff in the pack.

In bear country you will still have to cook away from your shelter and hang your food if you don't have a bear-resistant container. Pace out the right distance, making sure you can still find your way back to your shelter. (See pages 92–95 for more on bear-proofing your site.)

If you need a toilet, pace out the distance again—and take your flashlight with you.

Note these additional hard-won tips for dealing with the dark:

- Flashlight batteries don't last long unless you have an LED light, so use your candle or lantern, if you have one, as soon as you can.

- When packing flashlights and headlamp batteries, make sure they can't be accidentally switched on. If your light has an easy-to-press switch, remove or reverse the batteries.

- At night put your light beside your head so you can grab it quickly if you need it.

A stove windscreen will keep the breeze off a candle and act as a light reflector.

RAIN

If it's raining you'll want to erect your shelter as quickly as possible. If you've packed efficiently, you should be able to get your tent out of your pack without removing any other items. If you have to remove other gear from the pack, don't put it on the wet ground.

Once you've got your shelter up, leave your wet gear and pack in the porch or under a corner of the tarp and put on dry clothing; don't bring anything wet into the tent. Cook in the porch or the open side of a tarp so you can stay dry. In bear country pitch a tarp or ground cloth as a cooking shelter (when bears and wet weather are both likely, I carry a small tarp just for this). Be careful getting in and out of a tent in the rain. Squat in the porch if necessary while you put on or take off wet clothing. If it's cold *and* wet, get inside your sleeping bag as soon as you can.

If you use a separate ground cloth with your tent (which isn't necessary with modern tents) consider putting it inside rather than outside the tent; otherwise, rain can run between it and the tent groundsheet even if it's tucked in at the edges. With a tarp make sure that your ground cloth doesn't reach the edges so any runoff can drain into the ground.

STRONG WINDS

It may seem obvious, but when outside in strong winds don't let go of anything that might blow away. Keep gear in the pack or your shelter. As described above pitch your tent with the tail into the wind. Before going to sleep check that all stakes are firmly in the ground and all guylines are taut.

The noise of the wind or movement of your shelter may keep you awake. Sometimes just turning the tent around so the tail is into the wind can make a difference if the wind is hitting it from the side. A tarp can be lowered so it is only a foot or so above the ground. The wind whipping under it should keep it free of condensation.

If despite everything you can't sleep, distract yourself by reading a book, writing in your journal, or sorting gear. When dawn approaches start packing up so you can move to a more sheltered site as soon as it's light and maybe sleep part of the day.

SNOW

To pitch a tent on snow, first stamp out a flat platform and then wait while it hardens. If the snow is too soft for stakes to hold, put them in horizontally with the guyline wrapped round them and stamp them into place. The snow will soon freeze, and you'll probably need an ice ax to hack the stakes out come morning. You can also use skis, ski or hiking poles, or ice axes as stakes, or fill stuff sacks or plastic bags with snow, tie the guylines to these, and bury them.

Don't leave anything lying on the snow, as it could be buried. If the snow is deep enough, you can build a snow wall to protect your shelter from wind; you can even dig a snow "kitchen" with benches and a table. The warmest place to cook is in the tent porch, though, as you can lie in your sleeping bag.

When heavy snow falls, make sure it doesn't build up and collapse the tent. Every so often knock it off by banging on the walls from inside. Ensure you have ventilation, too: leave the top of a zipper or a high vent open in case snow seals the bottom edge of the fly sheet.

When getting in and out of the tent, brush as much snow off you as possible and throw out any that does creep in before it has a chance to melt.

Alternate Methods for Securing Guylines In the Snow

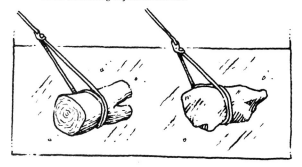

guyline tied around heavy log

guyline tied around a rock buried in the snow

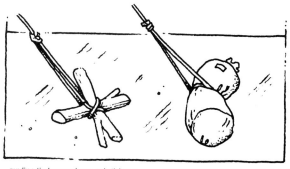

guyline tied around crossed sticks or stakes that are then buried in the snow

guyline tied around snow-filled stuff sack buried in the snow

FREEZING TEMPERATURES

When the temperature drops below freezing you may need to wear all your clothes to keep warm. If you're still cold, get in your sleeping bag. So you can use your arms, pull the bag up under your armpits and tighten the top draw cord so it stays there. (For how to stay warm while hiking, see page 32.)

During the night try the following if you feel cold:

- Have a hot drink before going to sleep.

- Do up your sleeping bag hood and shoulder baffle.

- If you wake up feeling chilly, don dry clothing, including socks and a hat.

- Spread extra clothing, such as a down jacket or rain jacket, over your sleeping bag for added insulation.

- If you only have a three-quarter length insulating mat, put clothing under your feet.

Protect your water supply from the cold. Bring water bottles into the tent and insulate them with clothing or put them in the bottom of your sleeping bag, if you're sure they won't leak. Tighten lids securely and then turn bottles upside down so any ice forms at the bottom, not the top. You can also empty water into your pots in the evening and then thaw it over the stove in the morning.

Wet gear, particularly boots, can freeze overnight. Bring wet boots into the tent, in a stuff sack or trash bag (turned inside out) so they don't dampen anything else, and cover the bag with spare clothing. You can also store the boots in your sleeping bag—this ensures they won't freeze, but it's not that comfortable. Place frozen boots in the sun in the morning; they should thaw fairly quickly. If it's not sunny, place a bottle of hot water in each boot to thaw them a little. If you have to wear frozen boots, don't put them on until you're about to start hiking. It isn't pleasant, but they'll start to thaw fairly quickly once you start moving. If you stand around in them, your feet will get painfully cold.

Protect battery-operated gear, as well. Batteries don't work well when cold. Store these items inside the tent, off the ground. If the batteries seem weak, take them out and store them in a pocket for a while or put them on a rock in the sunshine.

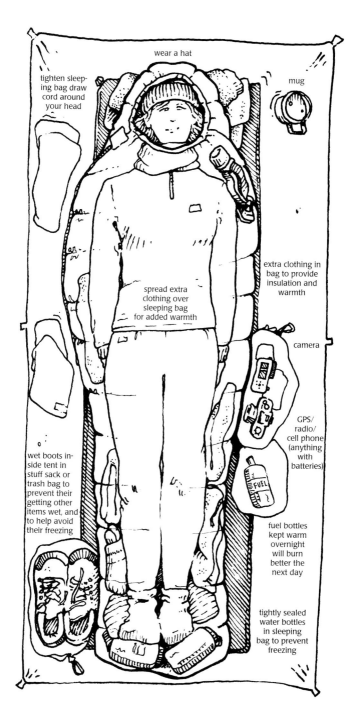

wear a hat

tighten sleeping bag draw cord around your head

mug

extra clothing in bag to provide insulation and warmth

spread extra clothing over sleeping bag for added warmth

camera

GPS/ radio/ cell phone (anything with batteries)

wet boots inside tent in stuff sack or trash bag to prevent their getting other items wet, and to help avoid their freezing

fuel bottles kept warm overnight will burn better the next day

tightly sealed water bottles in sleeping bag to prevent freezing

WATER, WATER EVERYWHERE

HOW MUCH WATER?

On a very hot day in open country you may need to drink a quart of water every hour. On a cool day in a shady forest a couple of quarts may be enough for many hours. A good practice is to drink small amounts often when hiking. Don't wait until you're feeling thirsty. By then you're already becoming dehydrated, and it can take quite a time to rehydrate. In camp drink plenty, especially before setting off in the morning. (Plain water is best for quenching thirst and rehydrating. Hot drinks may be nice when it's cool, but remember that caffeine is a diuretic: if you drink much coffee, it's best to drink even more water with it. Sports drinks aren't necessary for backpacking, and the sugar in them can make them sticky and not very satisfying.)

Always keep water handy; if you have to take off your pack to reach your water container, you might be tempted not to do so. Many packs have accessible, open-topped side pockets that hold a water bottle. A hydration system with a drinking tube lets you drink any time. (However, if the water container lies close to your back, the water can become unpleasantly warm.) In a group, help each other by getting bottles out of each other's packs.

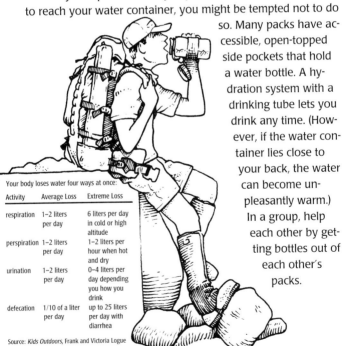

Your body loses water four ways at once:

Activity	Average Loss	Extreme Loss
respiration	1–2 liters per day	6 liters per day in cold or high altitude
perspiration	1–2 liters per day	1–2 liters per hour when hot and dry
urination	1–2 liters per day	0–4 liters per day depending you how you drink
defecation	1/10 of a liter per day	up to 25 liters per day with diarrhea

Source: *Kids Outdoors*, Frank and Victoria Logue

FINDING WATER

In all but the wettest areas you need to know where water sources are. In deserts this information is vital. Topo maps show creeks, pools, and springs, but they don't tell you whether they are flowing or whether they are seasonal. An up-to-date trail guide is a better source of information, but best of all is local knowledge. Before your hike check with rangers in the area about water sources, particularly if you're hiking where water might be scarce.

Where water sources are a day's hike apart or more, to reduce the amount of water you have to carry you can plan to arrive at the first source halfway through the day; have a long stop there, drinking deeply and perhaps cooking and eating a meal. You can then fill your water containers (treat before drinking—see pages 80–81), walk on, and camp halfway to the next water source. On hikes where water is really scarce, base your itinerary on water sources.

If you can't find one of your planned water sources, or you reach the location and the source is dry, use these clues to find water:

- In deserts and canyons look for cottonwood trees and areas of green vegetation.

- In rocky areas, depressions and hollows may hold water after snow or rain has fallen.

- In hilly country, go downhill from a pass or saddle, staying in the bottom of the valley, where water will flow.

- Stop and listen. Sometimes you can hear running water at a surprising distance; you might also find a faint seep that's nearby but hidden from view. *(continued)*

Water sources can be scarce on a hike.

- In deserts, water can sometimes be found in rocky creeks.

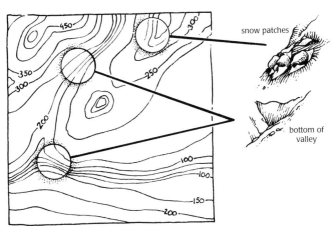

snow patches

bottom of valley

In any area look at the landscape and at the map for places where water might flow or settle, and search in those areas.

COLLECTING WATER

Collecting water is usually as simple as dipping a bottle into a source. However, if there is only a tiny seep or trickle available it can be difficult. First push the lip of a wide-mouthed bottle, a mug, or a cookpot into the water. Transfer what you gather into another container and repeat—it's slow, but effective.

To speed this process, create a channel for the water to flow along—this may be essential in places where you can't fit even the edge of a container. A small piece of plastic, foil, stiff paper or even bark can be used to direct the water.

If your water source is so far down in a hole that you can't reach it or in a creek below a steep bank, tie a length of rope to a bottle and lower it into the water. A few small stones in the bottom of the bottle will help it sink rather than bob about.

Take care not to trample and damage the area around the source. If you're camping nearby, fill enough containers for all your needs so you don't have to return to the water source. That way you won't disturb wildlife or create a side trail.

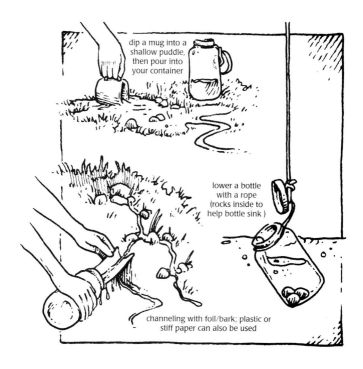

dip a mug into a shallow puddle, then pour into your container

lower a bottle with a rope (rocks inside to help bottle sink)

channeling with foil/bark; plastic or stiff paper can also be used

JUDGING WATER SAFETY

How can you tell if water is safe? You can't. You can only estimate how clean it might be. Water that smells or looks stagnant or mucky is probably not good to drink. But even water that is clear and fresh can contain *Giardia* or other organisms that can make you sick. (Clear water high in the mountains or deep in the backcountry is probably OK.)

If there are habitations of any sort (hiker's huts, ranger stations, ranches) above the water source (check the map for these) or cattle or horses or signs of them in the area, treat the water if you have to use it.

The safest approach is to treat or boil *all* your water (see next page). No treatment method is foolproof, however, so always take it from the cleanest sources available.

FILTRATION, PURIFICATION, AND BOILING

When you treat water, do it properly or it's a waste of time. Whichever water treatment method you use—filtration, chemical purification, or boiling—it's important that your hands are clean before you handle food or drinking containers. Wash them thoroughly after going to the toilet and before you collect water or cook. Failure to do this could nullify any water treatment. Keep water containers clean, too. There's no point dipping a clean bottle into a pool, treating the water in the bottle, and then drinking from the bottle. Use one bottle for collecting and treating water and then transfer the water to a clean container.

Follow water filter instructions exactly. Don't touch the filter unless your hands are clean. If your filter doesn't have a pre-filter unit and the water has visible debris in it, it's a good idea to filter this out first through a bandanna or coffee filter; otherwise it may clog your water filter. All filters will clog eventually; on long hikes carry spare cartridges or pack a chemical treatment as a backup. After use, clean and store filters according to the instructions. In the end, it can be difficult to maintain a filter properly on a long hike, and I would not want to rely on one.

Chemical treatments are much lighter to carry and easier to use than filters. Following the instructions is critical here, too. Chemical treatments take time to work, so you will have to wait as long as instructions indicate before you can drink the water. One disadvantage of iodine and chlorine is that they leave an unpleasant taste in the water. You can remove the flavor by adding ascorbic acid (vitamin C), but don't do this until the treatment has had time to work. Chlorine dioxide treatments, such as Aquamira or Pristine, don't leave a taste.

Bringing water to a boil is the most effective way to purify it, as all harmful organisms are killed before the water reaches the boiling point. There is no need to boil the water for any length of time. Boiling isn't practical for all your water but it's fine when you're going to use it for cooking. If you're going to drink boiled water rather than cook in it, shake it or transfer it from one container to another to aerate it, which will keep it from tasting flat.

Finally, if your filter fails or you run out of chemical treatments, don't risk dehydration by not drinking untreated water. You need water to continue hiking and to survive. If it makes you sick, you can deal with that later. (If you do get sick and it lasts more than a few days it's best to hike out and get medical treatment. In the meantime drink plenty, especially if you have diarrhea.)

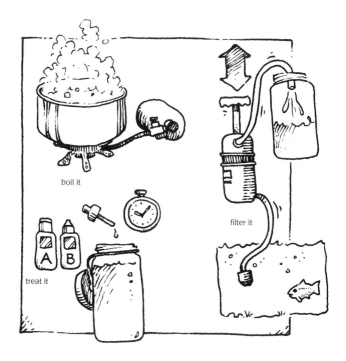

boil it

filter it

treat it

CAMPFIRES AND STOVES

CAMPFIRE BASICS

Light a campfire only if you can do so without causing any damage to the environment. Use existing fire rings where these are present to prevent the damage from spreading. On pristine sites look for bare mineral soil—sand or gravel—and dig a shallow scoop that can be filled in before you leave. Move aside any dead organic matter, such as pine needles and plant debris, and replace them afterward. You don't need a fire ring—just a foot or more of bare ground all around the fire.

If you have a fire pan, fill it with gravel or sand and place it on a surface that won't be damaged by heat.

Sand and gravel bars beside rivers or below the high-water mark on the coast are good spots for fires; the water will wash away all traces of the fire. Never light a fire on vegetation or organic soil. And never light a fire if it's windy—hot ashes could easily be blown about and start a forest fire.

Gather campfire fuel over a large area—don't strip every-thing immediately around your site. (If there is no firewood within a reasonable distance, it's probably a sign that too many fires have been lit in the area and it would be better not to light another.) Collect fallen wood that is small enough to be burned to ash. Don't bother with wood that is still green; it will produce a lot of smoke but not much heat.

To light a fire:

1. Start with a small, loose pile of dry kindling—scraps of waste paper, tiny twigs, small pinecones, dried leaves. Have plenty more kindling nearby to add to the fire if necessary. When it's *wet*, look for kindling in dry spots under logs and at the base of large trees. Slicing the end of a dry stick into a mass of fine slivers creates a feather-stick, which makes good kindling. If you can't find any dry kindling, add a candle stub or a solid fuel tablet to the damp stuff to help it burn.

  CAMPCRAFT

2. Build a small pyramid of dry twigs around the kindling, making sure there is plenty of air space.

3. Light the kindling and then add larger pieces of wood as the twigs catch.

4. Build the fire slowly—heaping on too much wood too quickly is likely to smother it.

There's no need to build a large fire. If you want warmth, sit closer—but remember that sparks will melt synthetic clothing. A small fire is more efficient for cooking, too. If you don't have a fire grill, don't balance your pans on rocks in the fire; this will blacken the rocks and is unstable. Instead, put your pan on hot ashes at the edge of the fire and heap hot coals around it. If you have a pot with a bail, hang it over the fire from a tripod of sticks. Keep a lid on unless you like ashes in your food.

Never leave a fire until it is completely out and the ashes are cool to the touch. If necessary douse the ashes with water until they're cold. Ensure that all wood is burned to ash. Scatter cold ashes, preferably over an unvegetated area, and then fill in the pit and scatter duff and forest litter over the top.

Dousing a Campfire

sprinkle water on the ashes

stir the coals with a stick and sprinkle again until no more steam rises

feel the ashes to be sure they're cool

scatter ashes over an unvegetated area

STOVE USE

You should be familiar enough with your stove before a trip that you can operate it safely when tired, in a storm, and in the dark. Always follow these guidelines for safe stove use:

- Make sure when you set up the stove that there is nothing flammable close by or above it.

- Before lighting the stove make sure all connections are tight and there are no leaks.

- When attaching a canister or filling a fuel tank or fuel bottle ensure there are no naked flames nearby. If there are, carry the stove some distance away before refilling it. A hundred feet isn't too far.

- Never overfill the tank. If there isn't an adequate air space in the tank, the stove won't pressurize properly and will burn erratically.

- Never cook inside the tent. If you're cooking in the tent porch (best only done in stormy weather or insect attacks) or under a tarp, refill the stove outside your shelter.

- When cooking in a porch, make sure the stove is well away from porch walls and the inner tent. Leave a porch door unzipped or, preferably, fully open.

- If you regularly cook in the porch or under a tarp, note that solid fuel stoves are safest for this, followed by alcohol stoves, then butane/propane canister stoves, then kerosene burners. White gas stoves are best used outside.

- Light white gas and kerosene stoves outside in case of flaring and then bring them under cover.

- When cooking in a shelter, make sure there is plenty of ventilation. Stoves give off poisonous fumes.

- Never have your head over a stove as you're lighting it or while it's burning.

- Never touch a stove until it has cooled down.

White gas and kerosene stoves need to be primed (preheated) before they will run properly. To light the stove, see the illustrations opposite.

Lighting the Stove

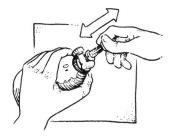

1. Pump the fuel bottle until you can feel firm resistance when you push the pump in—usually after about twenty strokes when the bottle is full. The emptier the bottle, the more pumping is required. It's easiest to do this before you attach the fuel bottle to the stove.

2. When the fuel bottle has been pressurized, open the valve a little until a teaspoon or so of fuel has squirted out and run down into the priming cup or onto the priming wick or pad. With stoves without a pump, dribble fuel into the priming cup from a fuel bottle with a pouring spout or an eyedropper filled from the fuel bottle.

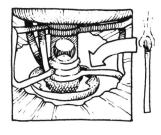

3. Light the priming fuel and wait until it has almost burnt out. Just before it does so open the valve; the stove should roar into life, burning with a blue flame. If the priming flame goes out before you've opened the valve use a lighter or a match; do this quickly, before the stove cools down. If the stove spurts yellow flames, turn it off; you haven't primed it enough. Wait for the yellow flames to die down then turn it on again. If it still doesn't light properly, turn it off, wait for it to cool, and then prime it again.

4. Once the stove is lit, let it burn for a minute or so at a low flame and then turn it on full. Don't turn the valve more times than recommended in the stove's instructions, or you could damage the connection with the bottle.

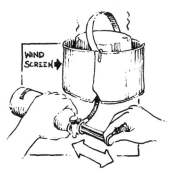

5. To maintain full power, pump a few strokes every so often. If you want a simmering flame, use the stove's simmer control if it has one, leaving the main valve on full. If there's only one control, turn it down to simmer and don't pump the stove again as it'll simmer better with low pressure in the fuel bottle. There'll be a short delay between turning a valve on the pump housing and the flame changing. Controls on the burner affect the flame immediately.

When you turn a stove off, don't wait for the flame to fade away. Blow it out so the final fumes can clean the jet. Don't dismantle the stove until it has cooled down. With some stoves you can turn the fuel bottle over and the last of the fuel will burn off, leaving a clean fuel line. With these stoves the bottle will depressurize, too, if you leave the control valve open. If your stove doesn't depressurize the fuel container, make sure you do this before packing it away so there's less likelihood of a leak. Point the fuel bottle away from yourself, companions, and equipment; when you release the pressure there will probably be a slight spray of fuel.

CARRYING FUEL

You can carry butane/propane canisters and well-wrapped solid fuel inside the pack, as there's no danger of them contaminating food or other gear. White gas, kerosene, and alcohol are best carried in an outside pocket. Fuel bottles are strong and unlikely to leak, but if they do these fuels can ruin food and damage gear. Always make sure bottle caps are firmly closed and that the rubber seals are in good condition. It's OK to leave a pump in a fuel bottle, but make sure you pack it so the control valve cannot be turned on accidentally.

STOVE TROUBLESHOOTING

If your stove starts to splutter and flare, perhaps going out altogether, the jet probably needs cleaning. Some stoves have built-in cleaning needles that you can operate by turning the valve in a certain direction while the stove is still lit. Other stoves have to be shaken to operate the cleaning needle. Turn the stove off before doing this and don't relight it until it has cooled down. A few stoves don't have a built-in needle; with these you need to carry one or, if you've forgotten or broken it, improvise—a toothbrush bristle is a good substitute. Remove the jet before cleaning it; otherwise you'll end up pushing any dirt down into the burner. If it comes back up in the fuel it may block the jet again.

If cleaning the jet doesn't work, dismantle the stove and clean the fuel line and generator if you can. Some stoves have built-in wires for doing this. On others you have to replace the generator if it becomes blocked. If you have this type of stove, carry a spare generator on long trips.

To avoid damaging O-rings, connect the parts of a stove gently and lubricate the end of the fuel line with saliva. Carry spare O-rings so if they are deteriorating you can replace them. Pumps have leather cups inside them that must be kept lubricated also, as the pump won't work if they dry out. Saliva is no use here. You need oil. Some stove maintenance kits come with small tubes of pump oil. Substitutes that work include lip salve, sunscreen, and margarine.

With some white gas stoves, simmering can be difficult. If this is a problem try pumping only a few strokes before lighting it and keep the fuel bottle no more than half full. Less pressure will mean a less powerful flame.

In cold weather butane/propane stoves don't burn very hot, especially when the canister is more than half empty. You can increase the heat output by warming the canister with your hands or insulating it by wrapping it in a piece of foam (cut from your sleeping pad if necessary). Insulate it from the cold ground by placing it on another piece of foam, a pan lid, or other flat item. When you're not using the stove, detach the canister and keep it in your clothing or sleeping bag.

No stove works well in wind. If you don't have a windscreen improvise one with a foam pad, pair of boots, stuff sack full of clothing, tarp, wall of rocks, large log, or other item. Always keep an air space between the windbreak and the stove. If the fuel container is situated below the burner, make sure any windbreak doesn't touch it and doesn't completely surround it. Check the fuel tank regularly to make sure it stays cool.

FOOD AND CAMP COOKING

THE CAMPSITE KITCHEN

Where you site your camp kitchen depends on whether bears are a potential problem or not. If they are, put your kitchen at least a hundred yards downwind from your shelter. Where bears aren't a problem you can cook where you sleep, setting up your kitchen next to your sleeping bag or just outside your tent or tarp.

The following tips will help make for an efficient kitchen:

- Keep your kitchen clean—food spills and drips will attract animals. If you do drop any food, pick it up and add it to your trash bag.

- When boiling water keep a lid on your pot—it'll boil quicker and save fuel.

- Use plastic or wooden utensils to avoid scratching non-stick pots. Metal utensils are fine with other types of pot.

- To keep food from sticking, stir it regularly and turn the stove down. This is especially important with thin stainless steel and titanium pots, which don't conduct heat evenly, leading to hot spots where food can stick and burn.

- When melting snow start with a bit of water in the bottom of the pot and add snow slowly—otherwise the snow may evaporate, leaving the pan to burn. Collect snow in a stuff sack or trash bag and dump it near your kitchen so you have plenty on hand.

- After cooking fill pots with water right away so food residue won't stick like glue.

- Wash pots well away from your camp and any water source.

- If you've been cooking over a campfire or using an alcohol stove, the base and sides of pots are likely to be black with soot. This can be hard to wash off. The answer is not to bother. Black pots conduct heat more quickly anyway.

  CAMPCRAFT

- Soft cloths and sponges are best for cleaning cookware, as they won't damage the surface. However, if food residues have cemented themselves to the inside and don't come off however hard you rub, sand and snow make good scourers (don't use sand in nonstick cookware).

- Strain out any food residues through a bandanna, metal strainer, or your fingers, put them in the trash and carry them out. Scatter wastewater in thick vegetation.

- Always wash your hands before and after handling food. And don't share eating utensils, bowls, or water bottles. Other people may not be as hygienic as you are.

Pack cookware in the heart of your pack where it is unlikely to be dented. If you'll need it during the day, the top of your pack near your back is a good place to carry it. Food and drink supplies can be stored inside cookware. To stop nesting pots rattling, a dish cloth or sponge can be jammed between them. Keep a cloth or piece of paper between nonstick pots, too, to avoid scratches. Many stove manufacturers suggest packing your stove inside a pot, but I don't recommend it—fuel smells can taint the pot.

The campsite kitchen is best located well away from your sleeping area. Set your stove on bare ground or rock so it doesn't scorch vegetation (this is especially important if the fuel tank or canister is set off to the side so the burner is close to the ground). On a well-used site there should be plenty of places like this. On a pristine site there may be none; here you can use a flat rock as a stove base (put it back where it came from when you've finished cooking).

WHEN AND WHAT TO EAT

Normal mealtimes can be abandoned in the backcountry. You should eat when you're hungry, which is likely to be often. Lunch may start soon after breakfast and go on until dinner. If you're starting to feel hungry stop and eat something. Continuing could mean running out of energy. And if you start to feel weary stop and eat something, even if you don't think you're hungry. It could be that you're running short of fuel.

In both cases what you eat should be primarily carbohydrates rather than protein or fat. Carbohydrates are what keep you going, the food that is most quickly turned to energy. Simple carbohydrates—candy, honey, anything sugar-rich—will give a very quick burst of energy, but this will probably be followed by an equally quick slump unless you also eat some complex carbohydrates—grains, legumes, vegetables.

If you run out of energy and feel you can't go on but you happen to be halfway up a steep trail and can't make camp, then stop, rest, and eat some carbohydrates. You'll probably be astonished at how much you recover. Energy bars, grain-based bars, oat crackers, bread, and granola are good carbohydrate foods, as is trail mix rich in dried fruit and seeds. High-carbohydrate foods (such as oatmeal, muesli, granola, and other cereals) are good for breakfast, too, giving you a high-energy start.

Fats—cheese, margarine, butter, oils, nuts—are digested more slowly than carbohydrates and take a long time to release their energy. Eaten in quantity during the day fatty food could slow you down, as it's not easy to digest while exercising. The best time to eat fats is in the evening; the slow energy release will help keep you warm during the night and keep you from waking up feeling hungry.

Proteins—meat, eggs, dairy products, grains, legumes—are needed to renew muscle and body tissue. Proteins are present in many foods. However, protein won't give you a sudden rush of energy, so high-protein foods are not ones to eat when you're tired and still have miles to hike.

Of course, everybody is different. If you find that a hunk of cheese gets you up the trail, then eat the cheese. If a high-protein or high-fat breakfast sets you up for hours of hiking whereas a high-carbohydrate one leaves you short of energy, then eat the breakfast that works for you.

SAFE FOOD STORAGE IN CAMP

Unless bears are a problem I like to keep my food with me overnight. Where no one has camped before this works well as animals don't expect to find food there. On well-used sites you may have a succession of visitors (mice and raccoons are two likely ones). This will certainly be the case if you leave your food some distance away from where you sleep but don't hang it. Having it next to you means that any raiding animal will likely wake you up so you can chase it away.

In some popular areas deer and other mammals may be a problem and food should be hung both to protect it and the animals—human food isn't good for them and plastic and foil can clog their stomachs so they starve. You are required to hang your food on some popular backcountry sites in order to protect the animals. The precautions needed in bear country aren't necessary, though—just hang your food from a branch high enough to be out of reach of deer.

hang food and garbage well away from your tent (see next pages)

PROTECTING FOOD FROM BEARS

Where bears may raid campsites keeping your food out of their reach is essential. Hang food at least 100 yards (90 m) from where you sleep and from where you cook (see instructions, opposite). If you use bear-resistant containers, store them that distance away as well. Leave them in an open flat area so that bears can't knock them down a slope or bang them against a rock or tree.

Containers are ideal for country where there are no trees big enough for food hanging. If you don't have a container all you can do in such places is split your food into a few bags and stash each one at least 100 yards (90 m) from each other and from camp.

Here are a few additional useful tips for bear-proofing your food:

- Some sites provide poles or wires for hanging food. Always use them unless you have a container.

- Remember that as far as bears are concerned food includes soaps, insect repellent, toothpaste, sunscreen, and other smelly items. Store these things with your food, along with any unwashed cooking and eating utensils.

- Food scraps and trash attract bears. Don't camp at dirty sites.

- The smell of cooking is a major attractant. To minimize the chances of a bear visiting your camp, don't cook and eat there. Instead, have dinner toward the end of the day and then walk on for several miles before you camp.

- In black bear country I don't hang food at pristine sites if they're at least a mile from popular sites and I'm not in an area with known bear problems, unless hanging food is mandatory. In grizzly country I do, as these bears are much more dangerous.

- If a bear does visit your camp and tries to get your food, make a lot of noise. If it doesn't go away, move on immediately or as soon as it's light enough. And if the bear does get your food, don't try to get it back.

If you haven't a bear-resistant container, you'll need at least 50 feet (15 m) of nylon rope to bag and hang your food from a high branch, out of the reach of bears. In some areas, including much of grizzly country, it is adequate simply to hang the food from a branch so it's at least 12 feet (3.5 m) above the ground, 10 feet (3 m) away from the trunk of the tree, and 6 feet (2 m) below the branch. To hang your food this way:

1. Put a small rock in a small stuff sack. Tie the end of your line to the sack and throw it over a branch about 20 feet (6 m) high. Don't let go of the other end of the rope! If you can't reach the rock, shake the line in a whipping motion to jerk the line over the branch and slowly lower the rock.

2. Grab the end of the line and remove the rock.

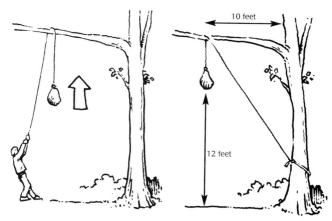

3. Attach your food stuff sack and haul it up.

4. Wrap the end of the rope around the tree trunk and tie it off.

Where the branches aren't long enough for the above method, you can suspend food between two trees about 25 feet (7.5 m) apart.

1. Attach your food bag to the center of the line. Attach a rock to one end as described above. Throw the rock over a branch and tie the end of the rope around the tree trunk.

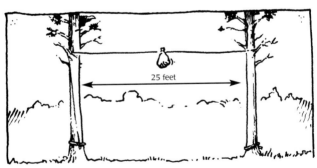

2. Throw the other end over a branch of the other tree.

3. Haul up the food sack and tie off that end of the rope.

CAMPCRAFT

In some areas with serious bear problems, such as Yosemite, neither of the above hanging methods will work, as the bears have learned how to get the food. Here you have to counterbalance food sacks, which means having both ends of the line at least 12 feet (3.5 m) above the ground and 10 feet (3 m) from the trunk of the tree.

1. Start with two stuff sacks of roughly equal weight. If you don't have enough food, put stones or gravel in one of the sacks. Tie one end of your line to one of the sacks.

2. Find a suitable branch then throw the other end of the line, attached to a rock as described above, over the branch and haul the first stuff sack up until it's just below the branch.

3. Tie the second stuff sack to the other end of the line while holding it as high as you can. Stuff any spare line into the stuff sack and then throw it upwards so that the two bags are at an equal height.

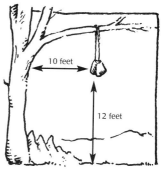

4. When you need the food use a trekking pole or stick to pull down one of the bags.

SAMPLE MEALS

The following is an example of what I usually eat on backpacking trips, long and short, summer and winter. I'm not proclaiming this as an ideal diet, but the food is lightweight and easy to prepare.

Breakfast: 4 ounces (115 g) muesli or granola with dried milk powder (mixed in at home). Simply add water, stir, and eat. You can add extra dried fruit, too. In cold weather, heat the cereal on the stove to make a sort of porridge. Keep the heat low and stir constantly or it'll stick to the pot.

Lunch: A series of snacks is better than one big midday meal for constant energy. A bag of trail mix or gorp is great for snacking. The basic ingredients are raisins and nuts, but you can add other dried fruit, sunflower and other seeds, chocolate chips, M&Ms, and granola. A couple of ounces a day should be enough unless it's the only lunch you carry. Oat-based grain bars are another good quick snack. For savory foods I eat tortillas or pita bread with cheese spread from a tube.

Dinner 1: 4 ounces (115 g) pasta per person (a type that cooks in 15 minutes or less is best), dried instant tomato soup (a pint packet serves two people) or tomato puree, 1 clove of garlic per person, mixed dried herbs, 2 ounces (55 g) hard

CAMPCRAFT

cheese (cheddar is good) per person, black pepper. Cook the pasta in just enough water. When it's done, without draining it add the dried soup powder or tomato puree (a tablespoonful per person should be enough), a pinch of herbs, and the chopped garlic. Stir well. Remove from heat. Slice the cheese and stir it into the pasta.

There are many variations on this meal. Add pesto (buy dried or in tubes or else transfer some from a jar into a small plastic tub with a lid that seals well) instead of or along with the tomato soup/puree. Add sun-dried tomatoes or other dried vegetables such as mushrooms and onions. Some people add tuna fish instead of cheese. You can also add dried milk powder as thickening and for extra calories.

Dinner 2: 3 to 4 ounces (85–115 g) quick-cook rice per person, dried vegetables (mushrooms, tomatoes, onions, peas), curry or chili powder, 1 or 2 tortillas per person. Soak the vegetables in enough water to cover. Without draining the vegetables, add them to the rice along with curry/chili powder to taste. Cook. Eat with the tortillas.

For variations, add textured vegetable protein or dried meat. Fresh garlic gives a bit more bite to the meal as can a splash of Tabasco sauce (tiny bottles are available).

FIELD REPAIRS

THE EASIEST PLACE TO DO EQUIPMENT REPAIRS is at home. Some repairs cannot be done at all in the wild. If you keep a note of any wear and tear while on the trail, you can do essential repairs before your next trip.

A few basic repair items can make all the difference when something goes wrong or a piece of gear is damaged. If necessary you can utilize other items of gear. Stuff sack drawcords can be used to tie things together. Adhesive tape from the first-aid kit can be used for patching.

BASIC MENDING

Rips and split seams in clothing and sleeping bags can be stitched up or, if the tear is a big one, patched. Don't worry what it looks like—as long as it holds together, it's fine. You can do a neat repair back home. A quick way to repair a small tear is to cover it with a piece of sticky-backed ripstop nylon tape or duct tape. This is great for repairing down-filled garments before you lose too much of the fill and repairing waterproof fabrics you don't want to stitch.

1. A ripstop nylon patch (or duct tape) sticks best if the surface it's applied to is clean. Wipe the area with an alcohol wipe if you have one (possibly in your first-aid kit for cleaning wounds).

2. Round the edges of the patch so they don't lift and peel off.

3. Once the alcohol has dried, apply the patch.

4. Press firmly on the patch until it is secure. If you have some adhesive you can use this to seal the edges of the patch as long as you don't mind the messy appearance, which may never totally disappear.

If you don't have the time or supplies to sew on a button, push a paper clip or twist tie through the holes and fabric and twist it together to hold the button in place. If a snap breaks, replace it with a button. Stitch around the edges of the holes where the snaps were to keep them from fraying.

ZIPPERS

Broken zippers can be a real problem. If it's a garment or pack zipper, an immediate short-term solution is to pin the sides of the zipper together with safety pins. This will get you to camp or a spot where you can stop and mend the zipper properly.

Treat zippers carefully and problems are less likely to occur. Yanking them open and shut, roughly tugging out caught fabric, and expecting them to work when dirty are all ways to hasten failure.

Here are some helpful zipper tips:

• When fabric gets caught in the zipper don't try and free it by jerking the slider. Instead pull the two sides of the fabric gently until the caught fabric comes out. A pair of pliers can be used for this or even tweezers on tiny zips.

• Zipper teeth can break, letting the slider part company with the zipper. If the gap is near either end of the zipper, sew it up or fill it with adhesive.

• If one of the stops at the very end of the zipper breaks off, stitch the end together to stop the slider shooting off the end.

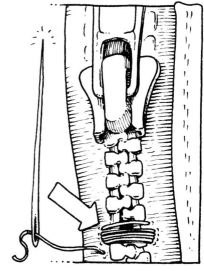

• Where teeth are missing in the middle of a zipper, causing it to separate, stitch the two sides of the zipper together. You'll be able to use only half the zipper, but at least it won't come apart. You can also stitch broken nylon coil zippers. *(continued)*

- Slider pull-tabs often snap off. Replace them with bits of cord, paper clips, or twist ties.

When you cannot repair a zipper in the field, use a length of adhesive-backed Velcro as a substitute. You might have to stitch the edges in place.

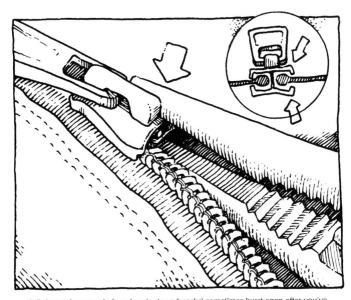

Coil zippers (commonly found on tents and packs) sometimes burst open after you've zipped them shut, due to a worn slider not gripping the coil tightly enough. Remedy this by carefully squeezing the slider with pliers. This is a delicate operation—squeeze too hard and you can smash the coils or over-tighten the slider.

FOOTWEAR

If you clean and treat footwear regularly and keep it away from heat, you shouldn't have too many problems. Don't dry wet footwear by a campfire or in hot sunshine—intense heat can cause leather to crack and soles to part from the uppers as glues dry out. You may just have to accept that you'll have wet boots for a while as they dry slowly on your feet. At night remove the footbeds so any moisture can escape and store the boots where animals can't gnaw on them for the salt from your sweat.

Boot Repairs

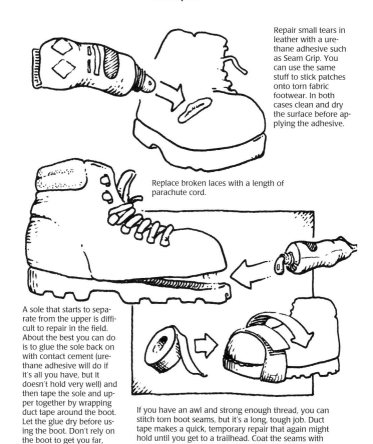

Repair small tears in leather with a urethane adhesive such as Seam Grip. You can use the same stuff to stick patches onto torn fabric footwear. In both cases clean and dry the surface before applying the adhesive.

Replace broken laces with a length of parachute cord.

A sole that starts to separate from the upper is difficult to repair in the field. About the best you can do is to glue the sole back on with contact cement (urethane adhesive will do if it's all you have, but it doesn't hold very well) and then tape the sole and upper together by wrapping duct tape around the boot. Let the glue dry before using the boot. Don't rely on the boot to get you far, though—just out to the nearest trailhead.

If you have an awl and strong enough thread, you can stitch torn boot seams, but it's a long, tough job. Duct tape makes a quick, temporary repair that again might hold until you get to a trailhead. Coat the seams with urethane adhesive to protect them against damage.

PACKS

Packs can get pretty beat up. These are the most likely pack repairs you'll run into:

- Plastic buckles break if you tread on them and may become brittle and crack in very cold weather. You can use duct tape for a makeshift repair, but it's better to carry spares so you can replace damaged buckles.

- You can stitch hipbelts and shoulder straps back on, too, if necessary. An awl and a strong needle are useful for this.

- Repair small tears and holes in the pack material with adhesive.

- If you have to replace broken or lost clevis pins on external frames, temporary replacements can be fashioned with wire and paper clips, though they don't usually last long. It's better to carry a few spares.

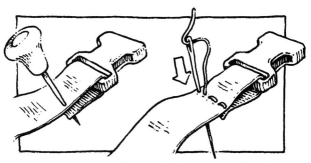

Stitch broken straps back together. (However, if one has ripped out of the pack, it's very hard work stitching it back in place. I'd do so in the field only if the strap was critical.)

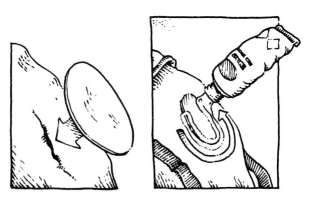

For larger tears, use a rounded (not square) adhesive-backed patch (see pages 98–99). Seal the edge of the patch with urethane adhesive so it won't curl up. Duct tape will do if you don't have any patches.

  CAMPCRAFT

- You can hold together a cracked frame with duct tape too, though again I wouldn't rely on this for long.

- Splint a bent or broken frame with a section of tin can or a stick and duct tape. The tin can be wrapped round the outside of the broken section, the stick jammed inside.

TENTS AND TARPS

Take good care of your tent or tarp—you're counting on it to protect you from the elements.

- If your tent or tarp seams leak in heavy rain, seal them with urethane adhesive. Don't use the tent until the adhesive is dry.

- Use adhesive-backed nylon tape to patch torn fabric, including insect netting and pole sleeves. Seal the edges with urethane adhesive. If the torn fabric has a waterproof coating, apply the tape to the uncoated side. Use duct tape for repairs if it's all you have. *(continued)*

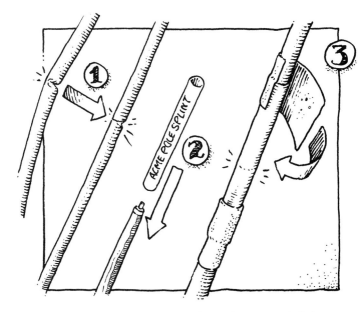

A pole usually breaks because you've stood on it, but sometimes a strong wind is the culprit. Most tents come with a pole splint; hold it in place with duct tape. If you don't have a pole splint, you could use a tent stake (curved ones that wrap round the pole are the best) or even a small stick. No repair will be anything near as strong as the original pole, so the broken section should be replaced as soon as possible.

- If a grommet or webbing loop starts to tear out or a seam comes apart, stitch it back together. Tape probably won't be strong enough at stress points.

- When the coating starts to peel off a fly sheet, ground-sheet, or tarp there's little you can do. You can cover small areas with duct tape or adhesive tape as a temporary solution, but you'll have to replace the item as soon as possible. Applying coatings or water-repellent treatments at home can extend the life of a coating, but it won't last long and I wouldn't rely on it.

SLEEPING BAGS

Repair a tear in a sleeping bag shell like any other nylon fabric: apply an adhesive nylon patch or duct tape (see pages 98–99). If it's a down bag do this very quickly, before too much of the fill has floated away.

For zipper repairs, see pages 99–100.

To stave off problems, dry damp sleeping bags in the sun. Air out down bags even on cloudy days as long as it's dry. If you can't air a bag in the morning because of rain or time, unpack it as soon as you make camp again and air it then. You can dry a really wet bag in front of a campfire, but be careful—sparks will melt holes in the fabric.

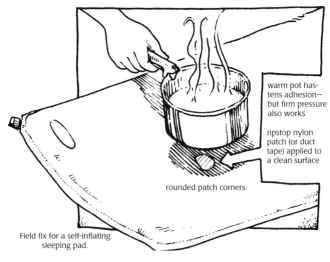

warm pot hastens adhesion—but firm pressure also works

ripstop nylon patch (or duct tape) applied to a clean surface

rounded patch corners

Field fix for a self-inflating sleeping pad.

SLEEPING PADS

The great advantage of closed-cell foam pads is that they're virtually indestructible. They do compress over time and can get ragged and torn but will still work.

Self-inflating mats are another matter because they can develop punctures. Here's what to do:

1. Find the leak. First, listen for the hiss of escaping air. Inflate the mat, close the valve, and then squeeze it tight while you listen. If you can't locate the leak this way dunk the pad in water, with the valve closed, and watch for bubbles escaping.

2. Once you've found the leak, clean and dry the area around it, squeeze out the air, and close the valve.

3. Apply a patch from your mattress repair kit. Make sure the patch has round edges.

4. Apply urethane adhesive to the patch edges to prevent them from peeling. (You can use duct tape, but it's not that effective and leaves a sticky mess that makes proper patching very difficult.)

Punch Bowl Falls, Oregon

HIKING POLES

A pole usually breaks at the tip, which is designed to be weaker than the rest of the shaft. You can go on using it if you don't have a spare tip. If a pole breaks higher up, use a tent stake as a splint and hold it in place with duct tape. Alternatively, jam a piece of wood inside the pole. For a strong repair, do both.

Sometimes an adjustable pole will collapse when you put weight on it. Usually tightening the internal expander on the section that has given way will cure this. Eventually these expanders will wear out and need replacing. Some poles can be adjusted with a screwdriver.

STOVES AND WATER FILTERS

For stove problems and maintenance, see pages 84–86. Most serious stove repairs are difficult to deal with and can't be done in the field.

Water filters need regular cleaning as per the instructions (see also page 80). The filter unit still may fail and will eventually need replacing, so carrying a spare is wise.

If the moving parts or the housing of a filter breaks, you could try repairing it with duct tape.

First Aid

FIRST-AID KIT

BACKPACKING IS A VERY SAFE PURSUIT. Minor injuries are unlikely, serious ones rare. However, it's wise to be prepared just in case.

There is no definitive list of what should be in a first-aid kit. For some good suggestions, see the first-aid kit checklist on pages 10–11. It is most important, though, that you know how to use every item—otherwise they're a waste of space and weight. You can use other items of gear in first aid as well: a bandanna can become a triangular bandage, duct tape can hold dressings in place, a foam pad can act as a splint.

A first-aid booklet will help remind you of techniques you studied before you hit the trail. You can always brush up on the information on rest days or during long evenings in camp. Taking a wilderness first-aid course is a good idea for all hikers.

The following is a brief outline of how to deal with some common, fairly minor ailments and injuries. It is not a substitute for more detailed knowledge and skill.

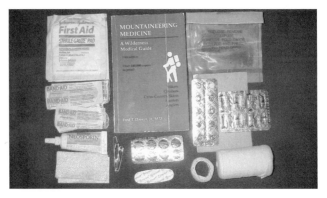

The Yukon, Canada

FOOT CARE

AVOIDING BLISTERS

If you commonly get blisters, you can tape those places in advance to reduce the chance of blisters occurring. In the long run, though, you probably need better-fitting footwear.

As soon as you feel a hot or sore spot on a foot, stop and investigate. If your socks are damp or matted with sweat, change them. If you stick with the same pair, turn them inside out and check for grit, grass seeds, bits of twig, rough seams, or anything that might be rubbing. Switching socks from foot to foot can make a difference, too. Put a dressing on the hot spot—adhesive tape, micropore tape, moleskin, or even duct tape will do. When you put your shoes back on make sure you lace them tightly. Slack lacing can allow your feet to move in your shoes or boots and rub against the sides.

Sometimes, though, the problem is too-tight shoes. If your shoes feel tight and your feet are hot, let your feet air for a while to cool them down and reduce any swelling. Take the insoles out of your shoes to make more room if necessary and don't tighten the laces too much. If you have lighter-weight footwear, hike in these instead.

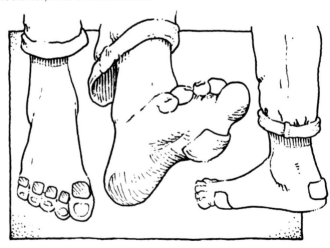

Common sore spots—put a dressing on them at first sign of trouble.

TREATING BLISTERS

When you get a blister—and most hikers do at some time—it needs treating. You're probably still going to walk on it, unless you can sit around for several days or more until it's healed, so it's best to burst it and then cover it with a dressing. For this you will need a sterile needle. If you don't have one in your first-aid kit, you can sterilize a sewing needle from your repair kit by holding it in a match or lighter flame. Here's the basic process for treating a blister:

1. Wash the area around the blister and wipe it with antiseptic.

2. Insert the sterile needle into the base or side of the blister.

3. Roll the needle over the blister so all the liquid is squeezed out, wiping it up with a piece of tissue. Squeeze out every drop, or the blister will be very painful when you start walking again. If the blister is large or under hard skin you might need several needle holes.

4. Once you've drained the blister, clean it with antiseptic, being careful not to break or move the loose skin covering it, as this protects the area while new skin forms.

5. Cover the blister with a gel that will cushion and help heal the blister, such as 2nd Skin or Compeed. You'll need to tape 2nd Skin in place.

When you resume hiking, the blister will probably feel painful for the first few steps. If the pain doesn't quickly ease off there is probably still some fluid in the blister; squeeze it again and put on a new dressing.

Blisters heal most quickly in the open air, so if they're really spoiling your hike you could take a few days off and sit around with bare feet until they heal.

ACHES AND BREAKS

SHOULDER ACHES

Aching shoulders usually indicate you're carrying too much weight on them. Try tightening your pack's hipbelt and loosening the shoulder straps. If just one shoulder aches, the strap on that side might be too tight. If loosening it doesn't help, too much weight could be pressing down on that shoulder; adjust your load accordingly. Hiking with a single staff or pole raises the shoulder on that side and may make it ache; swap the staff to the other hand every so often, or hike with two poles.

If you have a hiking companion, a shoulder massage can ease stiffness at the end of the day. You can also stretch and shrug your shoulders to release tension.

BACKACHES

Backaches can have many causes, none of them easily treatable in the backcountry. Carrying heavy loads on your shoulders isn't good for your back; keep most of your pack's weight on your hips. If your back aches, try tightening your hipbelt. Painkillers can help, and keeping your back warm is important. Sleeping on a hard surface is recommended for aching backs. This is not usually a problem for hikers! If you do suffer from regular backaches, use a firm pad rather than a soft one.

SPRAINS AND TEARS

A sprain is a torn ligament around a joint. It might be only minor, or it might prevent you from using that joint altogether. Treat sprains with RICE—Rest, Ice, Compression, Elevation. As soon as possible after a sprain occurs, treat the area with cold water, snow, or ice to reduce swelling and internal bleeding. Use an elastic or crepe bandage to compress the sprain and minimize swelling. Rest the injured limb, elevating it if possible, for as long as possible.

Sprained ankles are the most common sprains among hikers. When you have to walk out and can't wait for a mild ankle sprain to heal, there are two bandaging options to help support the ankle. One is to put a bandage in a figure-eight configuration over your footwear to help support it. The figure eight should go around the heel, under the sole of the foot, and across the top of the foot. Alternatively, you can wrap the ankle and foot with an elastic bandage, passing this under the foot and over the instep as well as round the ankle. In both cases, tighten the boot or shoe to give maximum support. A staff or hiking pole can be a great help as you limp along the trail. If you don't have one, find a stout stick.

The figure-eight configuration for wrapping a sprained ankle.

A severe ankle sprain requires evacuation. Walking will cause further damage and be incredibly painful. Also follow the RICE procedure.

A sprained wrist can be supported by a sling made from a triangular bandage or a bandanna, held in place with a safety pin.

A torn or pulled muscle is very painful and can be disabling. Treat the injury with ice or a cloth (a bandanna works) wrung with cold water, immobilize it, and see a physician as soon as possible. Torn leg muscles may mean you have to limp or even hop out. Again, a staff is a great help.

If an injury is too painful to even hobble on, it may be a fracture—see below.

BROKEN BONES AND DISLOCATIONS

Breaks and dislocations are serious and must be treated by someone with first-aid training. It is not within the scope of this guide to provide complete first-aid instruction that would allow you to tell a broken bone from a dislocation, but in an emergency it is best to overprotect an injury—that is, splint and wrap the injury to immobilize it (see illustrations). A proper splint immoblizes the damaged limb, prevents further injury, and improves the comfort of the victim. Materials to consider for rigidity in splints include hiking and tent poles, pack frames, or sticks and branches. Materials to consider for padding in the splint include foam cut from a sleeping pad, sleeping bag material, and extra clothing. Materials to consider for tying it all together include belts, bandannas, pack straps, and rope. You will probably need help to get out of the backcountry (see Evacuation, pages 132–35); then see a physician immediately.

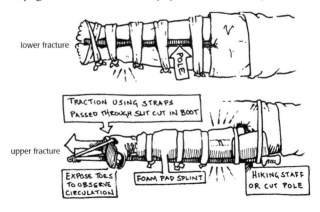

lower fracture

POLE

TRACTION USING STRAPS PASSED THROUGH SLIT CUT IN BOOT

upper fracture

EXPOSE TOES TO OBSERVE CIRCULATION

FOAM PAD SPLINT

HIKING STAFF OR CUT POLE

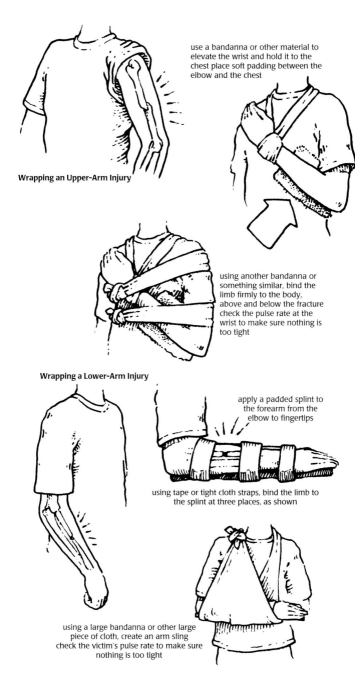

Wrapping an Upper-Arm Injury

use a bandanna or other material to elevate the wrist and hold it to the chest place soft padding between the elbow and the chest

using another bandanna or something similar, bind the limb firmly to the body, above and below the fracture check the pulse rate at the wrist to make sure nothing is too tight

Wrapping a Lower-Arm Injury

apply a padded splint to the forearm from the elbow to fingertips

using tape or tight cloth straps, bind the limb to the splint at three places, as shown

using a large bandanna or other large piece of cloth, create an arm sling check the victim's pulse rate to make sure nothing is too tight

HEAT AND COLD

SUNBURN

To avoid sunburn use sunscreen with a sun protection factor of 15 or more on all exposed skin. Apply it before you go into the sun and then several times during the day. Protect your lips from the sun with lip balm containing sunscreen. Note that the sun is strongest during the middle four hours of the day, so that's when protection is most needed. The sun is also stronger the higher the altitude.

A wide-brimmed hat or peaked cap with neck flap will protect the neck and shoulders. Tightly woven long-sleeved shirts and long pants will keep out the sun, but loosely woven garments won't. An umbrella gives the head and upper body great protection. For more on dressing for protection from heat and sun, see page 35.

When hiking on snow or pale rock or sand you can be burnt by sunlight reflected upward. Make sure you put sunscreen under your nose, ears, and chin.

If you get sunburned, cold, wet dressings, sunscreen, and moisturizing lotions can ease the pain. Keep the burnt area covered. If it's really sore you may need to put a dressing on it so it doesn't rub against clothing. If blisters appear, treat the sunburn as you would any other burn (see page 127).

HEAT EXHAUSTION (HYPERTHERMIA)

On hot sunny days a shady hat or umbrella will help keep you cool as well as prevent sunburn. However, the main cause of heat exhaustion, or hyperthermia, is dehydration, so drink plenty of water—more than you think you need. Keep an eye on your urine—it should be copious and fairly clear. Dark urine is a sign of dehydration (unless you've been consuming something that alters the color of urine, like beetroot or vitamin B supplements). If you start to feel weak or dizzy stop, find some

shade, and drink, drink, drink. However, too much water on its own can make you ill and can even kill you, so eat something, too, so you take in the salts your body loses during dehydration.

On really hot days, sit out the hottest hours in a shady place. If you do continue hiking, an umbrella with a reflective outer layer will keep out some of the heat. You still need to drink large quantities however and will probably find that you hike much more slowly.

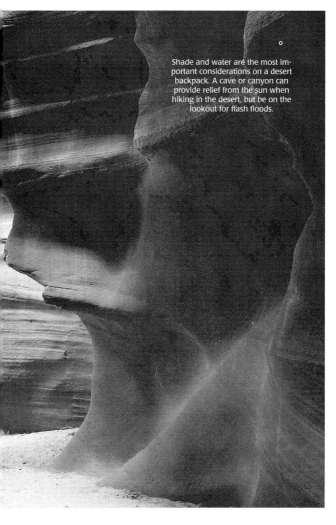

Shade and water are the most important considerations on a desert backpack. A cave or canyon can provide relief from the sun when hiking in the desert, but be on the lookout for flash floods.

HYPOTHERMIA

Hypothermia is a risk when you're both wet and chilled, especially if it's windy, and it can occur in above-freezing temperatures. To avoid hypothermia—which is when your body loses heat faster than it produces it—you need to keep warm and dry (see Staying Warm, page 32). Along with the right clothing, eating regularly and resting are important. You are more vulnerable to hypothermia when you're hungry and tired.

Hypothermia symptoms are shivering, lethargy, irritability, and lack of coordination. If you or any of your companions start to suffer from any of these symptoms, stop, set up camp, get into dry clothes and a sleeping bag, and have some hot food and drink. Don't move on until you feel fine again. If symptoms don't diminish, you'll have to evacuate the victim (see pages 132–35).

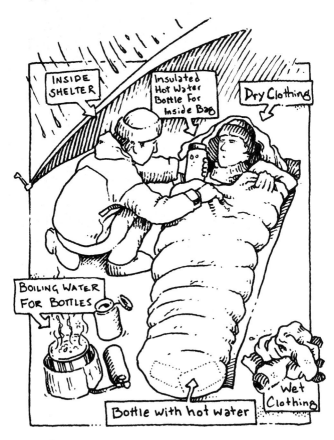

FROSTBITE

Frostbite is the freezing of body tissue. Keeping warm is the way to avoid it. Minor frostbite may occur on extremities—nose, ears, fingertips, toes—in very cold weather. The signs are numbness and a dull white, waxy appearance. Rewarm the area by putting on extra clothing, putting a warm hand over it, or, for fingers and toes, holding them in someone's armpit or groin or on their stomach. Don't rub frostbitten areas with anything, as this can damage the skin further.

Deep frostbite cannot be treated on the trail. With this flesh feels hard and blisters may appear on the skin. The skin becomes mottled with black and blue patches. This is a serious situation and the victim must hike out for medical treatment or be evacuated.

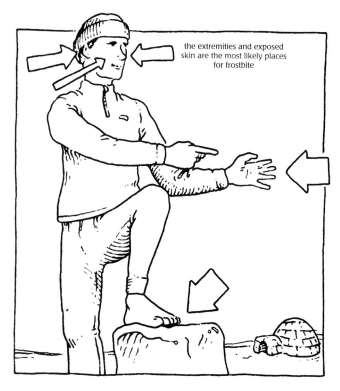

the extremities and exposed skin are the most likely places for frostbite

Yellowstone National Park, Wyoming

SNOW BLINDNESS

When hiking on snow for more than a half hour at a time, you need to wear sunglasses or snow goggles to prevent the sun burning your eyes and giving you snow blindness—which is very painful and disabling.

The first symptoms of snow blindness are soreness and irritation, followed by a feeling of having sand in your eyes. If this occurs stop and get into shelter as quickly as possible: if it gets worse you may not be able to see at all, perhaps for several days. Cold compresses and darkness can ease the pain, but beyond that you have to wait for your eyes to heal. Do not rub your eyes, which can damage them.

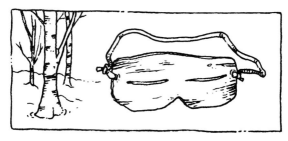

Two methods of constructing emergency snowgoggles. Top: Birch bark with slits. Bottom: Corrugated cardboard strips stacked and glued together.

OTHER COMMON COMPLAINTS

ALTITUDE SICKNESS

You might feel the effects of altitude above 5,000 feet (1,525 m), but altitude sickness (acute mountain sickness) is unlikely to occur below 8,000 feet (2,450 m). The symptoms are headaches, fatigue, loss of appetite, dizziness, and a general awful feeling. The cure is to descend. To avoid it in the first place, ascend slowly, spending a few days at 6,000 to 8,000 feet (1,825–2,450 m) before you go higher, and camp low until you are acclimated. Drink plenty of water, too, since dehydration can make the effects of altitude much worse. Acute mountain sickness isn't that serious and usually passes in a few days. However, high-altitude cerebral and pulmonary edema (fluid buildup on the brain or lungs) are both very serious and can be fatal. Symptoms include lack of coordination and noises in the chest. Distinguishing edema from acute mountain sickness can be difficult. If the latter worsens, descend immediately.

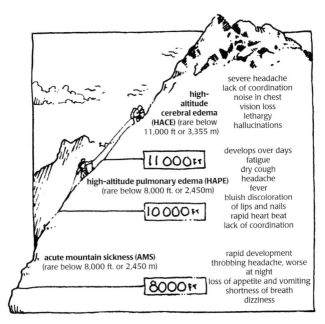

high-altitude cerebral edema (HACE) (rare below 11,000 ft or 3,355 m)

severe headache
lack of coordination
noise in chest
vision loss
lethargy
hallucinations

11 000 ft

high-altitude pulmonary edema (HAPE) (rare below 8,000 ft. or 2,450m)

develops over days
fatigue
dry cough
headache
fever
bluish discoloration
of lips and nails
rapid heart beat
lack of coordination

10 000 ft

acute mountain sickness (AMS) (rare below 8,000 ft. or 2,450 m)

rapid development
throbbing headache, worse
at night
loss of appetite and vomiting
shortness of breath
dizziness

8000 ft

CUTS

Clean a small cut thoroughly with water (and soap if you have it), treat it with antiseptic, and then cover it with a small dressing.

A severe cut also needs cleaning but will require a larger, thicker dressing. To prevent further bleeding, press down on either side of the wound with a bandage or thick cloth. Only press on the wound itself if it is completely clean and free from sharp debris.

If the wound is in a limb elevate it above the body. Use Steri-Strips or other wound closures to hold the sides of a shallow wound together. With deeper wounds, bind the edges together with bandages or strips of cloth.

Wrapping a Foot Wound

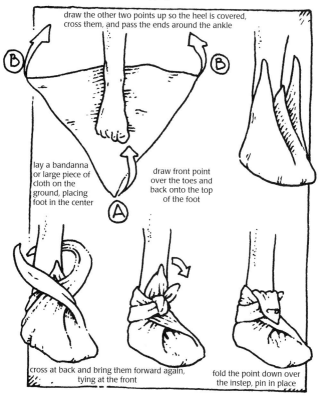

draw the other two points up so the heel is covered, cross them, and pass the ends around the ankle

Ⓑ Ⓑ

lay a bandanna or large piece of cloth on the ground, placing foot in the center

draw front point over the toes and back onto the top of the foot

Ⓐ

cross at back and bring them forward again, tying at the front

fold the point down over the instep, pin in place

Wrapping a Hand Wound

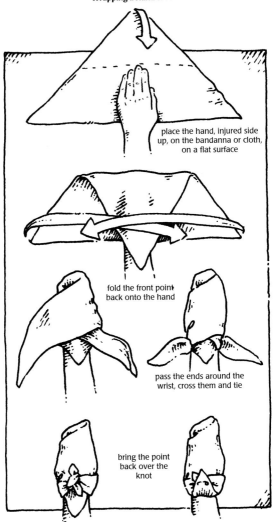

place the hand, injured side up, on the bandanna or cloth, on a flat surface

fold the front point back onto the hand

pass the ends around the wrist, cross them and tie

bring the point back over the knot

Wrapping a Head Wound

BURNS

Large, serious burns that cover more than 10 percent of the body are major emergencies that require very rapid evacuation (see pages 132–35) and hospital treatment. Give the patient warm fluids if he is conscious. Unless you can evacuate the patient very quickly, apply a large sterile dressing to protect against infection.

You can treat smaller burns in the field. But if you're not sure, get the person out. If the burn covers more than 1 percent of the body (about the size of the casualty's palm), the person should see a doctor, though they can hike out rather than requiring evacuation.

For a small burn, apply cold water for at least 10 minutes. If possible immerse the wounded area in clean, cold water. Otherwise, pour water on the burn. Cooling the burn down immediately is very important, so do this before removing the clothing covering the burn. Next, clean the injury and put on a gauze dressing. Don't burst any blisters that may appear. Don't apply soft dressings that could stick to the burn or greasy ointments. Analgesics such as aspirin or acetaminophen may ease the pain.

SNAKEBITE

See page 44 for tips on avoiding snakebites. If a snake bites you or a companion, there are a number of things you can do—and some you shouldn't.

- First, try to identify the snake. If the bite is from a nonpoisonous species, simply clean it and put a dressing over the wound. If it's a rattlesnake or other poisonous snake bite, venom may not have been injected. However, if there are puncture marks from the fangs and the bite starts to hurt and then swell, treat it as a poisonous bite.

- Don't use old-fashioned cut-and-suck snakebite kits or improvise anything similar—they can do more harm than the bite. Don't apply tourniquets, either. The only snakebite kit to use is a venom extractor (for example, Sawyer Extractor).

- After using the extractor, clean the bite thoroughly with soap and water and then bandage it and keep it at the same level or lower than the heart.

- The victim should be carried out or should rest while someone goes for help. Solo hikers will have to walk out.

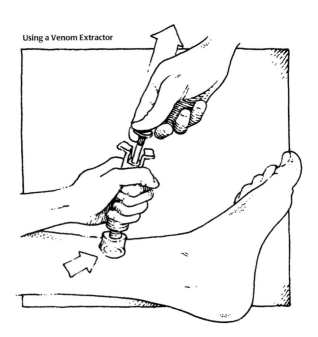

Using a Venom Extractor

TICK BITE

If you're traveling in tick country, see page 45 for help repelling ticks.

Ticks remain on the body for anywhere from two days to over a week, so you'll generally locate a bite by finding the body of the tick sticking out of your skin. If you find a tick embedded like this, grasp it at the mouth end with fine tweezers or a tick removal tool. Tug gently outward until the tick lets go. A tick removal kit containing magnifier, curved tweezers, antiseptic swabs, and instructions can be handy.

Ticks can spread serious illnesses. If you feel ill in any way in the few weeks after being bitten by a tick you should see a doctor. In particular watch out for a rash in the area of the bite.

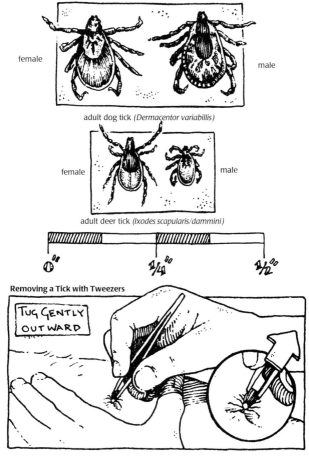

female   male

adult dog tick *(Dermacentor variabillis)*

female   male

adult deer tick *(Ixodes scapularis/dammini)*

Removing a Tick with Tweezers

TUG GENTLY OUTWARD

BEE AND WASP STINGS

If you're stung by a bee, wasp, or hornet you can use a Sawyer Extractor to remove the poison (and the stinger, if it's a bee sting). If you don't have an extractor, scrape the stinger out with the edge of a knife blade. An antihistamine can relieve mild allergic reactions like swelling and itching. A more serious allergic reaction must be treated with an injection of epinephrine, which can be carried in the form of an EpiPen (available by prescription).

SCORPION STINGS

If you're stung by a scorpion you can also use a Sawyer Extractor. Otherwise there's little you can do other than apply cold water or ice to the site to reduce the pain. However, stings from scorpions found in the U.S. are a serious threat only to the very young and the elderly.

SICKNESS

Stomach upsets may be due to pathogens in water you've drunk; contaminated food; dirty hands that came into contact with food, utensils, or your mouth; or even just the effects of traveling. Most will clear up in a few days. While the upset lasts, drink plenty, especially if you have diarrhea, to avoid dehydration—don't forget to *also* drink fluids other than water so you replace salts as well as liquid. If the diarrhea lasts a week, you should see a physician. However if you are in a remote area and are carrying Atabrine or Flagyl, antibiotics that kill *Giardia*, you could take a course of these in case you have giardiasis.

POISONOUS PLANTS

To avoid poison oak, poison ivy, and poison sumac, learn what they look like. Poison ivy and oak are easily identified by their glossy leaves, which grow in clusters of three. Poison sumac is found in marshy areas and is therefore usually not a problem for hikers. In areas where these plants grow, wear long pants and long-sleeved shirts. If you do brush against a poisonous plant and get the oils on your skin, you will probably suffer a very itchy rash plus a burning sensation and small blisters that can last a week or more. Some people have far worse reactions than others and require medical attention.

To treat this contact dermatitis, rinse the affected area thoroughly with cold water to try to remove at least some of the residue. Wash any clothing and equipment that has been in contact with the plants. Calamine lotion and a compress made from cloth wrung in salted water may relieve the itching.

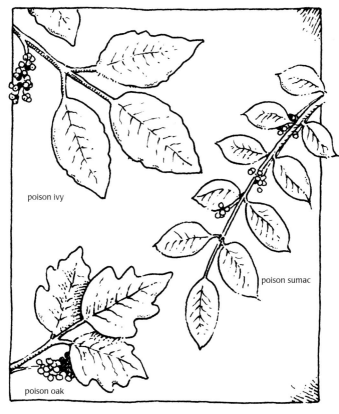

poison ivy

poison sumac

poison oak

EVACUATION

GETTING HELP

Self-rescue is always the ideal after an accident or when a member of the party is seriously ill. However, this assumes that the casualty can walk (or at least limp with the aid of hiking poles), that doing so won't seriously aggravate the injury or illness, and that the nearest trailhead isn't too far away. If the victim can't walk, other members of the party can transport them a very short distance (tens, not hundreds, of yards), again as long as this won't cause further harm. Realistically, if someone needs to be carried out and you're not very close to a trailhead, it's better for one person to stay with the victim and the others to go for help.

Write down crucial information for the designated person or persons to take when they go for help so that rescuers get complete information to execute an effective rescue:

- victim's age, health concerns, and current medication
- time of the accident
- full description of the injury (signs and symptoms) and how it happened
- action already taken to help the victim
- exact location of the injured person
- relevant compass bearings
- local features or landmarks
- nature of the terrain
- number and experience of the group

If there are only two of you hiking and evacuation is the only alterative, before you leave for help stabilize the injured person's condition and leave with them food, water, a watch, and a second copy of the list.

See pages 54–55 for signaling aids. Using a cell phone to call for help should be done only as a last resort; write down all the relevant details listed above before calling.

CARRIES

For very short distances two people can make a seat by gripping each other's wrists. You can also transport the victim on someone's back.

You can create a makeshift stretcher from trekking poles, insulating mats, and articles of clothing, but these are very uncomfortable and very difficult to carry—not worth bothering with unless there's no other option or you're going a short distance to a safer or more comfortable place. Even with a proper stretcher and plenty of people, carrying someone along a trail or over rough ground is hard, slow work.

cradle carry for
small children

human crutch—when victim can walk
(e.g., sprained ankle)

piggy-back—only when
conscious

firefighter's carry

FIRST AID

fore-and-aft carry

four-handed seat (when victim can use arms): each helper grips his own left wrist with his right hand, helpers link up; patient sits on helper hands as shown

Index

Numbers in **bold** refer to
pages with illustrations